20-Minute Vacations

Quick, Affordable, and Fun "Getaways" from the Stress of Everyday Life

Judith Sachs

A Stonesong Press Book

CB
CONTEMPORARY BOOKS

Library of Congress Cataloging-in-Publication Data

Sachs, Judith, 1947–
    Twenty-minute vacations : quick, affordable, and fun "getaways"
from the stress of everyday life / Judith Sachs.
        p.   cm.
    Includes index.
    ISBN 0-8092-2493-3
    1. Stress management.   2. Relaxation.   3. Stress
(Psychology)—Prevention.   I. Title.
RA785.S23   2000
155.9'042—dc21
                                                        00-20508
                                                        CIP

*For my father, who taught me to appreciate
each precious moment.*

Cover and interior design by Amy Yu Ng
Cover illustration and interior clip art copyright © Image Club/Eyewire
Interior illustrations copyright © Meredith Hamilton

Published by Contemporary Books
A division of NTC/Contemporary Publishing Group, Inc.
4255 West Touhy Avenue, Lincolnwood (Chicago), Illinois 60712-1975 U.S.A.
A Stonesong Press Book
Printed in the United States of America
International Standard Book Number: 0-8092-2493-3

01   02   03   04   05   06   QM   15   14   13   12   11   10   9   8   7   6   5   4   3   2   1

ᴗ: Contents :ᴗ

✌ Acknowledgments ✌

I am greatly indebted to Stephanie and Werner Mendel and the staff of the New Age Health Spa for their inspiration and encouragement.

This book was also given infusions of energy by Judith Berger, Susanna and Guy DeRosa, Valerie Kull, Marian Srokosz, and Johanna Walsemann.

Thanks, too, to Alison Fargis and Paul Fargis of The Stonesong Press, and my editor at Contemporary Books, Judith McCarthy, for shepherding this book along its path.

◡: Introduction :◡

Vacation. The word itself is almost enough to lower your blood pressure. Maybe you see it as a time to relax—lying on a sun-soaked beach with only the sea, sand, and palm trees as companions. Perhaps you like to be pampered—enjoy a full-body massage, followed by a delicious gourmet meal, followed by a long soak in a hot tub. Or you may view it as a time to strip down to the essentials—taking a backpack, tent, and canoe and communing with nature. Whatever you choose, this rest from work and everyday pressures is something to which you undoubtedly look forward with great pleasure and anticipation, even if it lasts only two weeks.

But it's hard to hold out that long! For the remaining fifty weeks a year, there's *Twenty-Minute Vacations*: more than enough getaways to make every day calm and stress-free.

We are a nation of workaholics. In the past ten years, Americans have added 164 more hours a year (a full month's worth) to their work schedule, and vacation time has shortened by 14 percent. Even if we do manage to escape for a few weeks, cell phones, voice mail, faxes, and E-mail keep us tethered to our jobs, no matter where we are on the globe. Many people feel guilty if they don't check in with the office at least once a day while they're away. How can we relax and unwind with all that stress hovering over us?

The answer is that no one should relegate vacation time to just two weeks a year. As with any activity, you need constant practice and experimentation in order to get good at it. And that's what you'll get with this book—the opportunity to take one or even two vacations a day, delicious bites out of your busy schedule when you can unwind and, for a moment, stop the crazy pace of your life.

This isn't easy. I was recently in an airport in West Palm Beach, Florida, about to return from a long weekend with a friend's family. We boarded the plane and were ready for take-off when the pilot announced that he had started his engines and only one of them was viable. He thought it would be a good idea to *de*board us until the fix-it crew arrived. Those passengers who had to make connecting flights would be accommodated if possible on other flights. We returned to the gate to wait, and, the rest of us direct fliers looked on in envy as our colleagues departed the waiting area.

The remaining natives, I noted, were growing restless. A flurry of cell phones were pulled out of carrying cases; some travelers petitioned the reps for a flight—any flight—that would take them anywhere on the eastern seaboard. Tempers flared. People pounded on the counter and raised their voices in protest.

And yet, there was another contingent of deboardees who seemed enormously content. It was OK for these folks to be stranded in the airport because there was nowhere else to go. My friend Maggi took out her guitar and started entertaining the kids. As the strains of "Old MacDonald Had a Farm" wafted through the airport, and children danced and turned cartwheels, smiles began to appear on several adult faces. Groups of people hung out in a circle on the floor and traded travel war stories. A woman did tai chi in the corner. These individuals calmed down. They breathed. An hour later, we were told that the engine needed a new starter, which would be driven down from Orlando because there were no available planes to carry it.

Seven hours later, we boarded the plane again. There was a marked difference in the two groups of individuals bound for home. Those who had allowed the experience to overwhelm them looked exhausted, frustrated, and in need of a stiff drink. The other half had made friends, laughed and shared experiences, and looked . . . well, as if they'd just had a seven-hour vacation. Whatever it was that was waiting for them at home had waited. They could get to it tomorrow. They were making the best of a difficult situation and staying in the moment. And that had made all the difference.

A break from the daily grind can actually make you a more productive and a more optimistic individual. When you give yourself the gift of a minivacation once a day, you have the opportunity to get some badly needed perspective on your stressors. Is it that important to make that phone call right now, this instant? (You'll probably just get voice mail anyway, so it doesn't much matter whether you call now or twenty minutes from now.) Is every piece of work—at the office and at home—a life-or-death issue? And if it were, wouldn't you rather approach it from a mental state that is fresh, calm, and harmonious, rather than one that is harried, anxious, and desperate?

✸ How to Use This Book

When you begin taking your much needed twenty-minute vacations, you'll probably want to choose a point in your day when you have a small window of opportunity—maybe when you first wake up in the morning, or when you're just home from the office or on the weekend. These vacations will serve as little breathers before you're hit with the onslaught of responsibilities and obligations. As you get better at snatching those precious minutes for yourself, you'll be able to take them when you most need them—when you're feeling pressed and rushed. Of course, this is exactly when you think you can't spare the time for a getaway. And you will vacillate back and forth— I can't spare the time; I must spare the time.

Look at it this way: you make the time to go to the bathroom, to do your makeup or shave, and to take a shower every day. Those are necessities. So, when you begin to think of time reserved for yourself as just as crucial, you've won the battle. If you're running late anyway, another twenty minutes won't make or break a deal. You can always call before embarking on this brief journey and say that you've been slightly delayed but that when you arrive, things will doubtless go swimmingly because you happen to be in a forward-thinking, terrific mood.

And then, stop feeling guilty. Go over the list of choices, and see what strikes your fancy: Do you want to experiment with something relaxing, a little wild, something to feed your soul or something that's just plain fun? Do you want to do it outside or inside? Do you want it to improve your mind, or do you want to veg out and let your brain be mashed potatoes?

Some of these vacations require planning, while others can be spontaneous. Most can be done alone; many will be a lot more fun with a partner. You can do some when you're sick but not sick enough to spend the day sleeping. You can do them in the middle of the night when you can't get to sleep because you're worried that you haven't accomplished enough the previous day and will have so much to do the next.

When and how you choose a particular trip will say a lot about you and the amount of stress you're trying to manage in your life. We live in a universe that is made up of the natural world, the world of technology, and the incredibly complex world of other people's needs and emotions. All we ever get to see of this world is our own little piece, looking out through our own eyes, judging by our own experience. So, the more we can expand our vision of what's possible and doable, the richer our time here on earth will be. Something as small and insignificant as a brief respite on some kids' playground equipment can teach us to think like a child again about the joyful delirium of zooming down a slide; something as important as reading a story to a child or examining the music of one composer will allow us to thank the powers that be for putting us right here, in the thick of the action. What a world!

Twenty-minute vacations alleviate stress because they are completely removed from those lockstep patterns in which we've been marching for years. It is much more difficult to agonize over whether your taxes are going up when you're rolling down a hill or meditating on the balance of two rocks of unequal weight. You have to concentrate solely on the experience you're having right then, right now.

In order to feel as if you are really on vacation, you have to turn off your mind, temporarily drop your obligations, and open yourself to new experiences. You have to seize the opportunity for a few minutes to yourself and guard it jealously from those who would whip it away from you. Of course, that's hard to do.

But everyone has twenty minutes to spare to do something relaxing. These minibreaks can make the difference between burnout and an even keel.

The best thing about twenty-minute vacations is that they never get boring. When you've had enough of one, you just move on to the next. In this book, you'll find 100 getaways in ten travel-related categories. They take so little time that you'll actually gain a few hours in your week just by doing them and then meeting the challenges of your day in a far more relaxed and positive spirit.

CAUTION: Getting into the swing of twenty-minute vacations might encourage you to linger. If you find that your allotted time is stretching to thirty or even forty minutes once in a while, congratulate yourself! Your practice is becoming ingrained, and the many benefits you've achieved from learning to treat yourself well will, in fact, teach you to manage time better when you go back to work.

If you actually *do* go back to work . . .

1
Inside Out

*T*here are times when you don't have the energy to explore new worlds. You want a lazy vacation all by yourself where nothing is expected of you. The ultimate in relaxation is suggested here—think, "veg out."

1 ❧ Nap It Up

The point of a power nap is to give your conscious mind a break. It doesn't matter if you don't fall asleep, although with practice, you may learn to relax sufficiently so that you do doze off for a few blissful minutes.

Try this at a time of day when there aren't a lot of people demanding your attention and the office or house is relatively deserted. Lunchtime is best, since the place should be pretty empty and the phone pretty quiet.

To start with, close the door, turn off the phone, adjust the shades, and dim the lights. You may want to put a Do Not Disturb sign on your door.

Take off whatever clothing is binding or pinching (jacket, belt, shoes), and clear a space on the floor. In order to get the feeling that you're really going to sleep, you'll probably want to put a pillow under your head and a throw over your body—you can store these in a drawer.

Before getting too comfortable, imagine a clock: see the current time pictured on it, and then move the hands forward twenty minutes. If the day is sunny, keep this mental clock well lit; if it's cloudy and dark, keep it in shadows in your mind. This suggestion will help you to end your twenty-minute vacation just when you want to.

Lie down and stretch out on your back, even if you don't customarily sleep on your back. Close your eyes, let your feet fall where they may, and rest your hands by your sides, palms up. Take a deep breath and enjoy it, relish it. You are now going to start with your toes and work your way up your body, telling each part of it to relax. Understand that by the time you reach your scalp, you will be lightly, comfortably asleep.

Let your breath do most of the work. As you scan each body part, encourage your breath to get deeper and fuller. Feel as though you are floating off the floor, carried by strong wings that protect and support you.

When you've finished your body scan, you may want to curl up on one side, or get into a position that you normally assume when you tuck yourself in at night. You may want to focus on one word, such as *peace* or *one*, or you may want to visualize the warm sun kissing your face and body.

Whatever you do, keep your mind on your breath—how even and regular it is. You can hear the inhalation and exhalation getting more expansive and more comfortable. You can take all the time you want and need. Now, *shhh* . . . .

After your nap, you'll wake refreshed. Slowly come back to consciousness. Stretch, yawn, and open your eyes. See how much better you feel: ready for the rest of the day. Ready for anything.

2 ❧ Mail-Order Dreams

The catalogs come in like clockwork, maybe three a day. Around Christmas, of course, you can't even get the mailbox open, there are so many. If you had the time and money, you could order clothes, shoes, household supplies, and vitamins; you could get chew-bones for your dog or an ergonomic chair that would heal your aching back.

Most of us just chuck the catalogs into the recycle bin the minute they arrive, and then find ourselves in the middle of the day, too harried to read a book or magazine, just aching for a quick glance through fantasy land. Here's the way to use those catalogs for a great twenty-minute break.

When the mail comes, set aside the catalogs that have terrific pictures or that entice you. (You can do this on-line if you don't happen to receive many catalogs by mail.) Don't worry about the price of the items shown—you're not going to buy anything—be concerned only with a look that holds your interest. Don't think about flipping through the pages until you're ready to embark on your vacation.

When you decide it's time for your mail-order vacation, grab a handful of catalogs from the pile. You are going to take a trip into the world that the catalog shows you. In the first five minutes, change your look. Those expensive clothes and jewelry fill your eyes with color and pattern. They may be elegant and luxurious or cheap and chic—it doesn't matter. Put yourself in the picture: see yourself wearing items that you might never put on in real life.

What about a catalog that helps you refurnish your house? In the next five minutes, you can start to plan a totally new living environment. You can see yourself surrounded by new styles of decor that would utterly change the way you live and the atmosphere of the place you live in.

In the final ten minutes, skim through several catalogs quickly. Why do some of them grab your interest and some leave you cold? Is it the subject matter? Is it the way you see yourself as opposed to the way you see the world embodied in this catalog? How much do you define yourself by the "things" you have, and how much by the type of relationships you develop, or the sense of yourself that you project to others? How many things that you currently have around you could you easily do without?

If mail-order dreams make you envious, take a moment to ponder what you think is missing. You may be surprised to find that whatever it is, it doesn't have a price tag. And as you come to this realization, you won't need to actually have the things on those pages—they'll just be there for you as an escape from the everyday grind.

3 ❊ Breath of Life

Inhaling and exhaling—you probably aren't even conscious of those precious breaths that occur over and over during the course of each day and night. You can turn this involuntary physical activity into a meaningful twenty-minute vacation that will get you in touch with the deeper sense of yourself that you probably ignore most of the time.

Find a place you like: it may be a corner of your living room, or out in the sun on a warm rock or on a ledge of a pool in front of an office building. Get as comfortable as possible and lie down. Loosen your belt and take off your shoes. You want your head in line with your neck, the chin slightly tucked in.

Let your shoulders go slack, draining into the floor or ground under you.

In order to breathe—really let go and breathe!—you have to allow the stomach muscles to release. Just for a minute, hold your breath, and tighten everything, from your pubic bone to your xiphoid process (the small bone beneath the sternum). Now let it out with a huge sigh. Roll your head from side to side, yawning as you do so. Oĸ, you're ready to begin.

It's important to become aware of the way you breathe normally, something of which you probably were never conscious. So, start your vacation as an observer of the process. Watch what happens as you take breath in and let it out. Do you breathe quickly or slowly? Are your inhalations and exhalations even, or does one take more time than the other? Do you stop and catch your breath, then inhale some more? Do you draw your nostrils closed, in an attempt to take in more air? Does your chest rise as you do this? Do you pause after you've exhaled, getting ready to breathe again? Do you hold your breath? Do you sigh a lot?

Don't judge yourself or decide that your breathing is "wrong" or "right." You're on vacation and you should be enjoying yourself. As you get deeper into the process, you'll find that it becomes easier and easier to fill and empty all the various cavities of your body—not just your lungs, nose, and mouth, but also, if you can imagine them clearly enough, your heart, your liver, and your bones.

Breathing should come right from your belly, don't worry about your lungs—they'll get oxygen no matter what you do. Put your hand on your lower abdomen, and push against it with your stomach muscles, as though you were pushing the air out. Then release your hand, and let the air come back in. See your belly as a balloon, expanding and growing as you inhale, deflating as you exhale. Be sure you inhale and exhale at the same pace, in the same rhythm. Loosen all your limbs, and allow them to be stirred by your breath. Breathe in and out through your nose, keeping your mouth lightly closed.

For the next part of this vacation, breathe normally, which probably will give you rather shallow breaths (this is the way most people breathe most of the time). Then, as your belly opens up and you are able to take in more air, let the breaths deepen and intensify. If at any point in this vacation you feel lightheaded or dizzy, just go back to your regular breathing.

Now you are going to get creative with your breathing by dividing it into three parts. In the first part, inhale into your belly just a little; then bring the air up into your chest, and finally all the way up into your throat. When you have as much air inside as you can possibly take, begin the three-part exhale: first, let the air out from the throat, then from the chest, then from the stomach. Continue this pattern as long as it feels comfortable. You can always switch back to your normal breathing at any point if the three-part breathing is too intense.

While you are on this vacation, you are going to think of nothing but the breath—how cool the inhalation feels as it rushes in through your nostrils, how warm the exhale feels on your upper lip as you let the air escape. The gentle in and out of breathing is like a wave, never really ending and never really beginning. There is always just a little left in your lungs, even when you've exhaled completely, and always a small gap at the top when you think you can't take in any more.

Your thoughts doubtless will stray in the midst of this journey; if you find yourself thinking about anything else at all, simply acknowledge the thought, let it go, and return to your focus on the breath. You want to feel like a passenger in a car, watching the scenery go by, enjoying each view but attaching to none.

A twenty-minute session of breathing will leave you refreshed and relaxed, ready for the rest of your day.

4 ❋ Looking Inward

Sometimes, keeping your feet in the air is more important than keeping your feet on the ground. In this vacation, which you can take in the office or at home, you're going to reverse your physical alignment in order to take the load off of your muscles and tendons. You can also get your blood pressure to ease back down from its usual peak.

The only equipment you need is a blindfold to block the light. You can use a handkerchief or scarf or any piece of cloth (preferably dark) that you happen to have around.

Close the door and turn off the phone. Tell those near and dear to you that you need twenty minutes of privacy. Take off your shoes, loosen your belt, and you're ready to begin. Lie on the floor and elevate your legs, propping your feet on the wall or door in front of you. Your knees should be slightly released, not locked and not bent. Place the scarf or cloth over your eyes.

Begin to relax by enjoying the darkness. There is nothing to see, nowhere to go. You'll find that your other senses are heightened. You may be very sensitive to sounds outside your room or office, you may be aware of different odors around you, and you will feel every vertebra in your spine as you sink deeper into the floor. You may find that you are flooded with memories, or you may find that your mind is completely clear, with no intention of concentrating on anything at all. Now as you relax your eyes, look inward. With the lids shut, imagine that you are looking upward at a point somewhere between your eyebrows.

Visualize a spot at the crown of your head. See that point opening up. Now you are going to begin to draw up the various tensions that you feel in your body and pull them right through that opening. When you have cleared out the debris, you can welcome in the positive energy coming from all around you. Feel it melting down, incorporating itself into your system.

Mentally close up that point that you have opened at the top of your head. Feel that your whole body is lighter; your feet are barely able to stay resting on the wall. You can now remove the cloth from your eyes and allow light to permeate your eyelids. Gently allow your eyes to relax open, and bend your knees, curling them into your chest. Roll onto one side, and then slowly sit up.

When you feel ready, come up to a standing position. Check your body and mind and see how different they feel from before you embarked on this voyage. Now you can go back to whatever you were doing with a clearer mind and a lighter step.

5 ❋ Pine-ing for a Vacation

You probably take trees for granted, but you won't after you take this vacation with a fine-leafed friend as your companion. Trees are wonderful role models for those of us who lack patience or can't tolerate minor frustrations. If you want to admire something, pick out one tree to spend time with and learn to emulate all its good qualities.

This vacation will help you to examine where you fit in the big scheme of things. Of course, as Homo sapiens, we think we're on top, but in fact, other life forms have a lot to teach us. Trees, for example, have it all over us in terms of time on Earth. They've seen things that we can only imagine.

Trees are majestic, long-lived, and impervious to some of the worst weather. If they're evergreen, they never lose their foliage; if they're deciduous, they may appear nearly dead in the winter, but to our surprise, they come back year after year, to leaf and flower again. Their roots keep them tied to the earth; their trunks never waver, yet their branches sway in the gentlest breeze. If we could be more like trees, we'd feel stable and secure, yet flexible— able to change direction at a moment's notice.

In this vacation, you're going to adopt a tree as your mentor and guide. Any tree will do, it shouldn't take long to select one, even if you're in a city where the pickings are slim. The one you want can be a shy, thin example locked into pavement on a busy street or hiding out in a small park. Of course, if you live in the suburbs or the country, you may have your choice of thousands, out along a quiet road or in the midst of your very own suburban sprawl.

For the next twenty minutes, you're going to have a conversation with this tree—not with words, but with attitude and aspect. First, see what its posture is like. Is it straight or leaning? Does it branch out from near the base, or does it rise up for many feet before dividing for the first time? Try to make yourself stand just like the tree: plant your feet about shoulder width apart, pull up your spine, and let your head rise toward the heavens. Let your body feel firm, yet movable. You should be able to sway and rotate around your roots (your feet, that is).

How big is the tree? The size of its trunk and its height will tell you if it's a fledgling grower or an old wise one who's been around for decades. Think of your own age and size: do you appear younger or older than your years? If you want to stump the guessers, you need to start acting like a tree. The taller you stand, and the more awareness you have around your trunk (your body, that is), the younger you'll look.

Now examine the foliage. Is it dense and tight, or can you see space between the leaves and branches? Are there buds or flowers? Does the tree have a distinctive aroma? Is this tree home to squirrels or birds that hide within its leafy bower? Think about your own personality as your particular foliage: Do you show yourself off or hide? Are you comfortable in your environment, and does it make your talents blossom? Do you mentor others and give them a place to relax if they want to?

The more parallels you can see between yourself and the tree, the more you'll find to explore. A tree is your mirror: take a good look, and admire what you see.

6 ❧ Chanting and Drumming

Hundreds of years ago, our ancestors celebrated by beating a drum and chanting. They might be grateful for a successful hunt, a new baby, or just the fact that the sun came up once again. Today, we tend to keep quiet and try not to draw attention to ourselves, but in this vacation, it's time to make some jubilant noise.

To lose yourself in this odyssey away from real life, you need rhythm. Slow, fast, syncopated, or on the beat, you are subtly drawn into an altered state of consciousness as you obey the regular count of meter. Paying attention to the beat, you can't fall back into old sluggish excuses about not having enough energy. The pound of your heartbeat will soon match the pound of the drum, whether you have a real instrument or not. If you don't have a drum, you can always use a table, a book, or a part of your body to keep the beat.

At the same time that you are drumming, you can also lift your voice in a chant. Chanting is unlike singing in that you don't need a melody (and it doesn't matter if you can't sing!). A chant is simply a sound that your voice produces over and over. It may be a slow, keening noise that emphasizes the deeper emotions inside just waiting to burst out. Or it may be a high-pitched celebration of being. It's useful to select a word that gives lots of opportunities for vowel manipulation, such as *oh*, *ah*, or *om*.

Start slowly, letting your hands keep a regular pace in their drumming. When you feel like letting your voice join in, listen carefully so that you can match the timbre of the drumming sound. Or you may strike up a descant above the beat, something that meanders and winds its own way like a rushing stream, moving from high notes to low ones, from happy sounds to sad ones. The good thing about this journey is that it's completely improvisational and will be totally different each time you take it.

While you're in the midst of this trip, keep your focus on sound. In addition to the drum and chant, you will hear other sounds around you: there may be noise of cars and machines coming from the street, or people talking or whistling, babies crying, birds singing, dogs barking. Whatever the sound, incorporate it into your vacation. Maybe you'll want to mimic some of the noises with your chant or your drum.

The performance is for you alone; no one else is there to hear or judge what you're doing. So, don't worry about what kind of sound you're producing and whether it's pleasing to the ear. Unless, of course, you have a partner who wants to play in the same band. In that case, you have the chance to expand the horizon of your composition and have twice as much fun as you would have on your own.

7 ✻ You Are Getting Very Sleepy

One of the best ways to get rid of annoying habits is through self-hypnosis. You can, of course, pay a hypnotist to help you stop smoking or biting your nails, but it's much more effective if you do it yourself. The patterns that our brains make—the ones that adapt us to certain habits—are ingrained, and we can change them only for a brief period of time with a suggestion from a stranger. But when we do it by ourselves, we've already made the effort to learn enough about motivation to alter our behavior. So, naturally, it works a lot better.

In just twenty minutes, you're going to do something so important that you will wonder why you never attempted it before. Hypnosis quiets the left side of your brain (the analytical) and leaves the right side (the imaginative) free to roam. You can make use of more alpha waves at this time, and those are the ones so vital during meditation. These brain waves can waft you peacefully into a new way of acting and being.

Just imagine: if your asthma is exacerbated by stress, you can calm it down, or if you've been criticized for interrupting when someone else is speaking, you can keep yourself quiet until it's appropriate to speak. The goal of self-hypnosis is to teach yourself to master your symptoms rather than expecting that they will vanish by themselves. At least 70 percent of all individuals are able to use self-hypnosis for healing—so, give it a try!

First, you're going to put yourself into a trance state. The technique, discovered by psychotherapist Herbert Spiegel, is known as the "eye roll." He found that simply rolling the eyes up into the top of the head so that the whites are visible could trigger a hypnotic state. The idea behind this is that the longer you look up, the heavier your eyes get, and the more they want to close on their own. This allows the brain to reverse what happens when you fall asleep. In fact, hypnosis lets you pay attention rather than drift off.

Start your twenty-minute session by lying on the floor or a mat and doing some deep breathing. Tell each body part to relax, starting with your toes and working up to the top of your head. Think about the particular behavior that you'd like to work on. Adopt a positive attitude toward it: you might say, "I'm ready to control my cigarette habit," rather than, "I *have* to stop smoking." When you're ready, tell yourself that you are about to begin the process of self-hypnosis.

On the count of one, allow your eyes to roll up.

On the count of two, take a deep breath and hold it.

On the count of three, relax as you close your eyes and imagine yourself floating. Allow the breath to become easy and natural. Feel that you are leaving the realm of dos and don'ts, shoulds and shouldn'ts. Let this floating feeling extend throughout your whole body. Suggest to your hands that they'd like to float up off the floor by themselves.

For the next few minutes, imagine yourself doing the activity or experiencing the feeling that you'd like to change. See yourself in the midst of it; then stop and run the picture backward, as though it were a videotape running in reverse. When the tape has run out, you will no longer have a desire to do, feel, or say whatever it is you're trying to eliminate from your life.

You will now take several minutes to affirm what you've just done. See yourself in many different settings, with different people around you, but minus the habit. Congratulate yourself for having succeeded in this work.

Finally, you are going to end your trance. On three, you will allow your eyes to roll upward in your head. On two, you will take a deep breath and hold it. On one, you will open your eyes and come out of your trance.

See what happens in the next few days: the habit may not be completely gone, but your need to repeat it may have lessened. The more you repeat this brief vacation, the more you will feel a great connection between your inside and your outside—and will know that you have the ability to change your own life.

8 ❧ A Write It Out

Keeping a diary or journal is one of the best and most profitable vacations you can take. It's a quick trip, but it will make you feel as though you've experienced a whole day with all its variations. More important, people who keep journals are found to be much better able to manage stress; writing offers a kind of therapy that can actually be better than talking to a friend or loved one.

A journal lets you explore your relationships with others. If you're angry, you can express it fully; if you've just fallen in love, you can wax poetic about the beauty, kindness, generosity, and sexiness of your darling. The greatest thing about keeping a journal is that you can be completely honest without fear of hurting anyone or compromising yourself—and how many of us do that consistently?

Something else you can do in a journal is overcome obstacles. You may find that you have been struggling to get through a particularly hard time—maybe you've just experienced the breakup of a relationship or the death of a parent or partner. In words, you can work out what's bothering you, and you can take steps to overcome the problems that seem so tough when they come at you full force.

A book of blank pages is a delicious gift that you can give yourself, although you need only a pad and a pen or pencil, especially if you take this vacation only once in a long while. Don't be intimidated by those empty pages that you have to fill; start with one, and see what happens.

How do you start? For many people it's tough to get personal right away, so the easiest thing to write is a list. For the first couple of minutes, warm up by listing whatever you feel you want to write about: things that make you happy, things that are eating at you, trips you'd like to take, movies you'd like to see. Relax your arm and hand and let the writing implement flow across the paper. Don't think too hard; just let the words form themselves before your eyes.

Read through your list, and see if there's some common theme here: love, travel, money, growing older—who knows what's been running through your mind? If you see something in the lists that you can grab onto, write a little about your feelings on the subject. If there's no theme evident, pick one of the items on one of the lists, and explain why it interests you.

Eventually, you want to get down to the core, to write about your most intimate feelings. That's when the benefit of this vacation really makes itself clear. Don't be afraid: say what you want to say. You may find that you weren't even aware of how lonely or frustrated you were, and at the same time, you may discover positive shades of yourself.

Enjoy the words. Read them out loud if you have time at the end. When you allow yourself to plunge into this vacation, you can emerge refreshed, revitalized, and filled with the love of language.

9 ✴ Candle, Candle, Burning Bright

One of the oldest meditative techniques involves focusing all your attention on a candle flame. Thousands of years ago, when our ancestors lived in caves and feared the dark, they spent their nights huddled close to fire. This not only kept them warm, but also protected them from predators and from their own superstitious fears that the sun would never rise again. You can give yourself the same type of comfort by simply lighting a candle and spending twenty minutes peering into its heart—the flame that keeps it alive.

A candle flame is beautiful, a white plume rising out of a blue base, with a hot yellow center. It wavers in the breeze but can remain quite steady, drawing the eye and the attention. There are all sorts of candles: fat and thin, short and long, aromatic and unscented. The best one to choose for this vacation is the simplest variety, one that appeals to you because it has some quality that you admire.

Sit quietly in a shaded or darkened room, and strike your match. Hold it in the air for a moment, seeing how the flame takes shape, then touch it to the wick of your candle. Watch the flame move from one side to the other, much like a baton being passed in a relay race. Now you can blow out the match and set it aside.

How close do you want to be? Give the flame room and oxygen to breathe. If you like, come in just a little closer to feel the warmth of the candle wax near your hand. Let your eyes focus directly on the flame. It will draw you in, almost without your wanting it to. As you breathe in, see how the little fire appears to draw near you; when you exhale, it will move away slightly. You will almost feel as though you two are dancing together, swaying with the movement of your breath.

Take time to notice the wax at the base of the flame. See how it softens and begins to drip. It has such a yielding nature; it doesn't protest as the fire melts it down. This is something to keep in mind when you feel as though the pressures of daily life are molding you, changing you in ways that make you want to fight back. Instead of putting up a stubborn front, let go, and see if your own strength can surmount the problem. When you don't put up a rigid exterior, people are more willing to move in your direction.

Depending on the air around it, the flame may subside and become very small, or it may peak and extend upward. You can fan it a little to make a change if you like. Let your eyes follow the flame wherever it goes, not expecting that it will lead you anywhere in particular. Whether it's large or small, it has an intensity and a stature that attracts you, making you feel part of its presence.

Now blow the candle out. As the smoke rises upward, feel your own body stretching out, the top of your head reaching for the sky. As the smoke curls and dissipates, understand that you have taken a journey that brings you to a place inside that you rarely visit. This haven of quiet and mystery is yours, anytime you want it.

10 ✖ Get Happy!

When Judy Garland opened her voice and her arms and sang, "Sing Hallelujah! C'mon, get happy! You're gonna chase all your cares away," the whole movie screen brightened. The generation who grew up during the Great Depression knew real sorrow and trouble—but somehow, they were able to look at the bright side when they went to the picture show and saw stars like Garland performing with an exuberance that made them want to jump up and sing with her.

If you're too young to think that Judy Garland has what you need to cheer up, try Bobby McFerrin's similar song, "Don't Worry, Be Happy." The easy, loping rhythm of this ditty, which came along in the '80s, made everyone feel better. And the classic feel-good song, of course, is Beethoven's "Ode to Joy." The power of a huge chorus belting out the phrases banishes the ability to feel blue or depressed. A lot of songs have this power to undo the knots of worry and let your own great feelings shine through.

On this vacation, you're going to sing along with your favorite happy piece of music. Find a tape or CD that unfailingly puts a smile on your face. If you don't have one, go out and buy one. Listen to the song all the way through, and figure out what it is about the lyrics and the music that makes your toes tap and your heart lighten. Maybe it's the driving beat that moves forward no matter what; maybe it's the ebullient performance, or the way the message is "sold" in the song. Pay attention to the singer, the way the timbre of the voice carries the sense of the words and makes them mean more.

Of course a lot of the conventional phrases in songs seem trite and simplistic: why, in fact, should we be able to stop worrying and just "be happy"? But sometimes by saying those words aloud, by acting *as if*, we can turn around a difficult situation. Even if you're feeling very down when you start this vacation, you can lift yourself a notch or two by the activity of singing. You have to breathe deeply, opening the chest and getting oxygen moving throughout the body, and you have to produce sound. It doesn't matter whether you have a good voice or a terrible one: what is vital is that you express the sentiment found in the song you're singing.

Raise your head! Open your mouth! Sing your heart out!

11 ❧ The Ups and Downs of Yo-yos

A yo-yo is an endlessly interesting toy, good for young and old. When you have one of those shiny plastic or wooden disks in your hand, you begin to feel the cares of the day rolling off you just as the yo-yo rolls off your fingers.

If you can take your yo-yo outdoors, so much the better. But anywhere will do, as long as it's sufficiently far from delicate glassware or your computer screen.

Place the ring of the string around your middle finger, and heft the weight of the yo-yo in your hand for starters. Cast out, letting the string unwind. Just as you're getting toward the bottom, reel in again. Let the yo-yo play nicely, in and out, up and down, without giving a thought to anything but the fun of playing. Keep your arm relaxed and elastic and the toy will bounce right back at you. If it doesn't, and it runs out to the bottom, don't be discouraged: wind it up and try again, this time with a little less forceful throw.

You can also do many fancy tricks with a yo-yo. One of the favorites is "Walk the Dog": curl the yo-yo in toward yourself and cast downward. As the yo-yo starts spinning on its own, let it touch the floor. You will see that it is propelled forward with its own momentum and all you have to do is follow it as you do your faithful Fido. (This is the perfect dog, who needs no cleanups and is always ready to move on, but nicely, without dragging you.)

When you've mastered that trick, you can try "Around the World": throw the yo-yo overhand (your palm faces the floor) straight ahead of you. As it gets to the farthest point, move your arm in a big clockwise circle. The yo-yo will fly around your body and back out again, from which point, you can snap it back into the palm of your hand.

If you find that you're not terribly coordinated, you can still take a yo-yo vacation. It's very pleasant to hold a yo-yo in your hand, roll it back and forth on your desk, and throw it up in the air and catch it. Who says you have to take the prescribed trip where you see five countries in four days! You can take the lazy version where you lie back and take it easy—and enjoy yourself just as much.

2
Pamper Yourself

You don't have to visit an expensive spa to partake of an aromatherapy massage, a salt scrub, or a pedicure. In just twenty minutes, you can make your home a luxurious sanctuary with the help of some ideas in this chapter.

12 ❧ A Date with Mr. Bubble

A bubble bath is one of the nicest ways to pamper yourself. Just the thought of it lightens your spirits (how could a bubble ever be heavy?) and makes you sigh with eager anticipation. A bubble bath should be relished and savored, but if you have only twenty minutes, so be it. Make sure you have your bath area prepared in advance, so that you can jump right in and start your vacation without having to do anything that will spoil the mood. Bubbles are widely available in body and bath shops as well as in drugstores. You can use Ivory soap, too, but it won't be as much fun.

The preparation is simple: turn off the phone, make sure the kids are happily engaged in a game, book, or video, and explain to everyone that you are not to be disturbed once you enter your sanctuary. We are going to assume that you have scrubbed the tub earlier in the day and laid out your loofah, nail brush, and sponge. You'll have an inflatable pillow for your head that sticks to the side of the tub, or else a folded towel to cushion your neck. If you don't have music in your bathroom, you will have moved the radio onto a secure, dry shelf, or brought in a CD player that changes disks automatically. There will be a whole set of candles, or perhaps one potent aromatherapy candle, waiting to be lit. You'll have poured yourself a glass of chilled chardonnay or a pot of herbal tea, and you will have fresh, clean, fluffy towels and a bath mat waiting for you when you get out. Run the water, and test it periodically to make sure it's not too hot, not too tepid.

Your date with Mr. Bubble is an exercise in pure hedonism. As you ease into the water, you want to smell the delicious bubbles rising up to meet you. Your body will slowly disappear as you sink beneath the surface. If you enjoy total immersion, go ahead—let your head sink, and feel the sensation of your hair slowly absorbing moisture. Under the bubbles, you are a mermaid or merman, dipping into the cool cave you call home.

As you come up for air, you will delight in the waves that lap against you. Look at your legs, so far away near the faucet, your arms rising up to take the washcloth off the hook. Take a handful of bubbles, and hold them up to the light to see the iridescent sheen of the airy baubles in your fingers. Feel what it's like to listen to music as your ears alternately fill up with water and empty again, so that the sound is muffled, then clear.

When you come up for a sip of wine or tea, you'll notice the wrinkled skin on your hands and around your nails, that raisin look that reminds us of what we were like as kids, when we would spend long summer days in the pool. In that long-ago time, we had no work that called us back, no obligations other than enjoying life. We needed to run, jump, and have fun. We had that innocent ability to sit on a rock in the sun or lie still in a quiet pool of water, just as we are now. We might almost be dissolving: muscle, bone, and tissue turning to pure liquid, and from there, to pure spirit.

Nothing to do. Nowhere to go. You have become a bubble yourself. Lighter than air, you float up toward the ceiling and linger there, grinning and shining.

13 ❧ Cool as a Cucumber

When you've had as much pollution as you can bear, when other people's cigarette smoke invades your space, when your eyes are itchy and red from examining too many annual reports, it's time to retire to a cozy, luxurious den of your own creation. This twenty-minute vacation can actually be taken in your office with the door closed, but you may feel more relaxed in the privacy of your own home.

You will need a few ingredients: a thick cucumber, a jar of honey, a bowl of ice, some body lotion or cream (drugstore variety is fine), a pair of large athletic socks or slippers, and a couple of those quick cold-to-heat packs from a drugstore—the kind you either put in the freezer or warm in the microwave.

Peel your cucumber, and make slices about 1/4-inch thick. Place these on ice. Warm the two packs in the microwave, take your shoes off, get some oversized socks or slippers, and you're ready. You may want to put a little classical or New Age music on the stereo.

Sitting on the couch, rub your hands and feet lightly with lotion. Place the hot packs into your slippers or socks, then slide the footwear onto your feet (which will be a little slippery from the cream anyway). They should feel toasty but not uncomfortably hot. Raise your feet on pillows so that they are level with your head. To keep your lips moisturized and soft, smear a teaspoon of honey on them, and put a cool cucumber slice on each eyelid. Then settle back, and feel yourself sinking into the couch. This is your time to be idle and indolent. You deserve it.

Cucumbers have a drawing effect: the cold will seep behind your lids and soothe those irritated orbs. You might want to put a couple of slices on your forehead if you have a headache. As the cukes lose their chill, just toss them aside and take fresh ones from the bowl.

The nice thing about this vacation is that you are pampered in so many ways. You can imagine invisible hands tending to your head, your hands, and your feet. You are cold from the cukes and warm from the hot packs. You taste the sweetness of honey on your lips. You can smell the nice clean scent of the vegetable and the more perfumed odor of the body lotion. You are in an optimum position so that your spine can realign itself and your tired feet can let the circulation return from whence it came—back to the heart.

You may feel yourself dozing off, which is perfectly acceptable. Or you can just allow yourself to relish the sensual delights of so many good things happening to you at once. It's actually hard to come back from this one after just twenty minutes. If you must, set an alarm, or indulge at the end of the day, or on Sunday when you don't absolutely, positively have to be anywhere at any specific time.

This is the life. And it's all yours.

14 ❋ Tea for One

If you go to any of the classy, expensive spas around the world, you'll be drenched in tea. Not to drink, but to steep your face in. One of the best and easiest ways to clear your sinuses and open your pores is to hold your head over a pot of chamomile tea.

Why chamomile? It's one of the oldest known herbs (the Egyptians dedicated it to the gods), and you can get it in any supermarket, bagged or loose. The name comes from the Greek and means "apple on the ground," and of course, all you have to do to evoke the experience of standing in an orchard in autumn is to smell it.

This herb is great for numerous things. You can use it if you feel agitated and want to calm down, if you have menstrual cramps, or if you're sick to your stomach. It's also used to make beer. And if you're not into drastic chemical dyeing, you can use it to lighten your hair. Because this herb is so versatile, it's a great buddy on a pampering vacation. This is a wonderful trip to take if you have a cold or cough. Inhaling the essence of the warm tea will help everything to flow and your lungs to unclog.

Put four bags of chamomile tea or a handful of loose tea into a medium-size pot of water and let it come nearly but not quite to the boil. Set the hot pot on a trivet or cork pad, and drape a bath towel over your head. Then position yourself over the pot so the steam can rise into your face. Stay a couple of feet away for the first five minutes. You won't be able to stand the heat when you begin, so you'll want to lift the towel away from the back of the pot. Your face will start dripping, as will your nose. Your eyes will sting from the salt tears being drawn out of them. Soon you'll feel the temperature moderating, and you'll be able to drop the ends of the towel. Now just hover over the pot and cook for the next fifteen minutes. Breathe in the apple essence; let it permeate your skin and your lungs.

When you emerge from your steaming, you'll be flushed and glowing. What a way to go back to work—everyone will want to know where you've been.

15 ✻ Skin Sensation

There is a kind of freedom to putting a lot of goop on your face and lying back to let it work its magic. You rub it into your cheeks, forehead, and chin. Then, in just a little while, the cream comes off, and the true you rises to the surface.

In fancy spas, cosmeticians and herbal wizards spend hours concocting potions that will cost you a fortune. Why not save the money and feel wonderful by whipping up these recipes at home? All the ingredients are available at health food stores and supermarkets. The few ingredients you'll have to get from a pharmacy will be in the prescription department, although you don't need a doctor's prescription to purchase them.

Following is a beauty regimen that will make you feel and look splendid. Each one takes about ten minutes to prepare once you have your ingredients assembled. That leaves you ten minutes more to apply and use them. I suggest that you start out with an oatmeal cleansing mask, nourish your skin with a fruit facial; then that night, apply night cream to soften your neck.

Oatmeal Cleansing Mask

½ cup oatmeal
juice of one lemon (or 2 tablespoons cider vinegar)
2 teaspoons plain yogurt

Work the ingredients into a paste. Rub the paste into your face, more vigorously on the forehead, nose, and chin, more lightly on the cheeks. Be extremely careful with the skin around the eyes and mouth. Allow the mask to sit for fifteen minutes. Wash it off with warm water and pat your face with a soft, dry towel.

Fruit Facial

Recent studies show that alpha-hydroxy fruit acids assist in the new growth of skin cells. But you don't have to purchase the high-priced cosmetic spread in a department store: all you need is a lot of fruit.

> 1 handful of strawberries, sliced
> 1 ripe peach, cut into chunks
> ½ cup canned pineapple chunks, drained
> ½ medium cucumber, peeled
> 1 egg white

Place all ingredients in a blender and combine them into a paste. Spread the paste over your face and neck. Relax for ten minutes, then wash off.

Night Is Right Cream

This lovely night cream will smooth away the cares of the day. All ingredients can be purchased in a health food store or pharmacy (without a prescription).

> 2 teaspoons beeswax
> 2 teaspoons lanolin
> 4 teaspoons almond oil
> 2 teaspoons distilled water
> Pinch of borax
> 2 capsules (1 teaspoon) wheat germ oil

Warm the beeswax, lanolin, and almond oil over boiling water until they have melted and combined, or place them in a microwave for a few minutes. Warm the distilled water, and dissolve borax in it. Allow both liquids to cool.

Mix the two liquids together, then beat in the wheat germ oil.

Note: You may add infusion of comfrey or marigold to help cell regeneration. These herbs are found in health food stores.

Nice Neck Cream

Don't you just hate those folds in your neck that you hardly notice in real life but that show up big as life on photographs? They make you feel like a turkey with wattles. But you'll enjoy the sensation of applying this delightful neck cream. See if you notice a difference the next time you have your picture taken.

1 tablespoon cocoa butter
1 tablespoon lanolin
½ cup peanut oil (or wheat germ oil)
3 to 4 tablespoons water

Melt the three oils over boiling water until dissolved. Add water in order to make the cream easier to spread. Allow the mixture to cool, then place it in a jar and refrigerate it. Shake the cream before use.

Note: The cream may appear cloudy.

16 ❧ De-Stress as You Self-Press

After a long day, do you ever rub those throbbing points in the muscles that connect your neck to your head? Or when your head aches, do you massage the indentations at your temples? If so, you have discovered acupressure, a centuries-old Chinese technique (related to acupuncture) of alleviating stress and tension by putting pressure on certain sensitive locations in order to clear blockages along the energy pathways of the body. In just twenty minutes, you can release tension by using those points that connect to your stress center.

In Chinese medicine, there are fourteen meridians, or energy pathways, which approximate the body's internal organs (although no one organ is ever targeted for treatment). The organ systems are: Lu (lung), LI (large intestine), Sp (spleen), SI (small intestine), Ht (heart), Ki (kidney), UB (urinary bladder), GB (gallbladder), and Li (liver). The other four systems are: Pe (pericardium), TB (triple burner), CV (conception vessel), and GV (governing vessel).

When you press with fingertips or knuckles on any point along one of these fourteen energy pathways, you can alleviate pain and, in addition, work on the immune system, the circulatory system, and the gastrointestinal system. You're also relieving muscle tension by allowing blood and oxygen to flow through your tissues to your brain. And you don't even have to leave your desk to take a vacation to a land of physical plenty and comfort.

Sit cross-legged on the rug, or sit in a straight-backed chair with your feet flat on the floor. Close your eyes, and begin to breathe in and out, paying attention to those areas that seem uncomfortable or tense. Reach your hands out in front of your body, and extend through the tendons and ligaments, as though you were trying to pull your arms away from your shoulders. Stretch the fingers wide, then allow them to release back; let the tension drain from your arms and shoulders. Rub your palms together for a count of twenty, and then hold them about an inch apart so you can feel the warmth generated between them.

In order to get relief, you'll have to work the acupressure points for about five minutes. Start gently, moving from the surface of the skin down through the layers until you reach muscle. Hold, then back out of the point slowly, releasing your pressure.

Unlike Western medicine, in which you can access the various muscles and nerves coming out of the spine and across the back when you massage the shoulder, acupressure points in Chinese medicine derive from meridians that may touch on both internal and external organs. Here are a few points that will help you alleviate general anxiety and tension:

Liver (Li) 4: in the web of connective tissue where the bones of the thumb join the hand

Urinary Bladder (UB) 10: two points on either side of the cervical spine at the atlas of the skull, where it meets the neck

Gallbladder (GB) 21: two points about four inches out from the spine, where the neck meets the shoulder

Urinary bladder (UB) 36: two points in the hollows at the top of the shoulder blades.

Acupuncture works on the basis of the gate theory, which postulates that there is close proximity in the brain for sensory

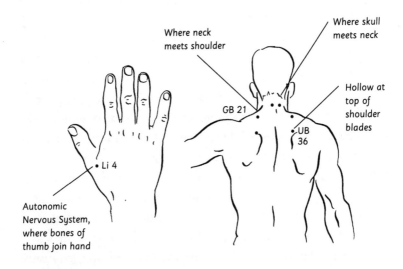

Acupressure Points for Stress

thresholds between pain and pleasure. When the pain gate is closed, it's impossible to feel anything but pleasure. Here is the one vacation that truly gives you the keys to the city—and you can open the gates all by yourself.

17 ❧ Paint the Town Red

Giving yourself a manicure or pedicure is a great way to let go of the customary tension in your hard-working hands and feet. This vacation allows you to pamper those parts of you that do so much and are often neglected.

Get all your equipment ready to start. You'll need an emery board and a clipper, a nail brush, a bowl or basin with warm water and soap, some cuticle remover, some orange sticks or a cuticle pusher and perhaps a cuticle nipper, massage cream, and a pumice stone for the calluses on your feet. You'll also need a towel and perhaps a few cotton balls or a tissue to wipe up spills. Turn on some music that appeals to the hedonist in you, and find a comfortable spot where you won't be disturbed for twenty minutes. Shine a good light on your efforts: this will lighten your mood as well as offer the best view of your labors.

Start by filing your nails to give them a new finish at the tips. You may clip toenails if you want, but be sure to run the file over them afterward so they don't snag socks or stockings. Fingernails may be as diversified as your personality—long elegant rounded ones, or neatly trimmed with just a sliver of white showing. Next, put those nails in a bowl or basin, and scrub the grime and dirt from beneath them—watch the suds foam around your hands or feet, and then rinse it off. Let them sit for about five minutes. Some of the nicer salons put marbles or flat river stones in the water so that you have something for your hands and feet to play with while you're waiting, and you may wish to try that at home.

When your nails feel slightly soft and the cuticles are manageable, pat them dry, paying specific attention to each finger or toe. Now you'll want to smear them with cuticle remover and start pushing the cuticles back. Be careful—if you work too forcefully or go too deep, it hurts, and it may damage the nail bed. Clearly, that's not the point of this trip. Everything should feel good to you: take it easy, move slowly, and watch how one hand cares for the other, or how both hands can care for your feet.

Some people like to cut the cuticles. If you do so, trim off only the excess. Look at the nails now—their pearly quality can shine as you manipulate the tools in your hands. Do you have a broken nail or one that's peeling? Instead of agonizing over the quality of your nails, think of them as parts of your life that need a little more attention. Nails, like plants, keep growing, and the more care and nurturing we give them, the healthier they are.

This is the time to lavish attention on those digits. If you're doing your feet, rub them between your hands and then use a pumice stone lightly to remove calluses. Both hands and feet would love a special massage; use cream liberally, and work it into all the dry areas. Wipe your hands or feet on the towel, and examine them. How different they seem now from when you began.

You may end the session with polish if you like, but if you have only twenty minutes it will have to be the speed-dry variety. Go wild with color: let it match your mood. Let your hands and feet tell a story about you—one that will keep you amused and relaxed, no matter what happens next.

18 ❧ Face It, You're Beautiful

Many women dash out of the house in the morning with barely enough time to apply a little lipstick and mascara. And during the day, as the makeup fades or is rubbed away, we tend to stop looking at ourselves in the mirror and concentrate on work, work, and nothing but work.

But there's nothing more pleasant than looking your best. Most department stores will do a complimentary makeover for you in the hope that you will purchase their products. The beauty consultants are generally knowledgeable about color, shading, and skin texture and can complete your transformation in twenty minutes or less. Think of how much fun this will be. It doesn't matter if you have a hot date after work or will just be going to pick up your kids and then home to start dinner.

The way you look very often affects the way you feel. You probably know how terrible you appear to yourself if you have a slight cold or cramps or a headache. The "you" whom you see in the mirror may not be different to an outside observer, but the image may strike you as a vision of discomfort. Similarly, if you're looking wonderful, you can sometimes get through the toughest experiences with self-confidence and bravado.

So, on your lunch hour or after work, get yourself over to a makeup counter. (Find out in advance what, if anything, you have to buy to get this free service.) Decide what image you want to play with—you don't have to look like yourself every minute of every day. It might be fun to ask for a different look—more sophisticated than usual, or more sweet and innocent. You might want to get dramatic evening makeup, or something unmeltable that you could wear to a garden party on a summer day.

Explain your preferences to the beauty consultant, and hear what he or she has to say. Then sit back in the chair, and give yourself over to the ministrations of the expert. For the first five minutes, relish the touch of the consultant's hand, the cream and tissue that remove your old makeup. You can be completely vulnerable, letting someone else reframe the vision of yourself that you usually monitor so closely. Once you're relaxed, spend the next ten minutes paying attention to what the consultant is doing. Notice the order of the products being applied, how the brushes feel on your face. Let this be a purely sensual experience, and revel in the odors of the creams and lotions being rubbed into your skin. Feel that you have begun to glow from the inside out, just as you are taking on a new image from the outside in.

Finally, the last step is to look at yourself—really look. See the vision of yourself all made up, and then see through it. What is it about your face that you enjoy the most? Is it your sense of mystery or your openness? Is it your flair and energy, or is it the cool, quiet facade that hides the emotions within? Allow the makeup to enhance the person within, and enjoy yourself looking as you do.

19 ✷ Heaven Scent

Just by smelling the cookies baking in your grandmother's kitchen, you felt happy. When you caught a whiff of that freshly cut grass from your backyard, you knew your father was home and all was right with the world. Locating our personal happiness and recalling important times in our life by scent is known as aromatherapy.

We are guided by smells far more than we think. The area of the brain responsible for processing scent is located in the limbic system, the emotional house of the mind. In addition, the scent center and the memory center are adjacent to each other in the limbic system. So, if we connect up with an odor that suggests a wonderful memory or an anticipated event, we can shut out the difficult or boring facets of everyday life.

In just twenty minutes, you can change your whole aspect with the right scent. You may use aromatherapy candles in strategic places in your home or office, or essential oils, if you're not allergic to them. These oils are derived from plants and offer both medicinal and emotional benefits. You'll have to experiment with a few different ones to find what works for you. Then, too, you'll want different scents for different occasions, depending on the effect you'd like to have on your mood. Here is a brief menu of some aromatherapy possibilities:

Try **bergamot**, **geranium**, and **ylang-ylang** to treat depression and anxiety.

If you're agitated and need to calm down, try **Roman chamomile**, **neroli**, or **patchouli**.

If you feel hopeless, try **jasmine** or **mandarin**.

If you have zero energy and need to perk up, try **orange** or **peppermint**.

If you're distracted and can't concentrate, try **frankincense**.

The oils for complete relaxation are **sandalwood** and **ti-tree**.

The oils are very versatile. You can put a few drops in your bath, use them as a component of a massage oil, or keep them next to your bed in a diffuser throughout the night.

But let's assume you would like to relax completely in the middle of a busy day. If you're at the office, you can take a sandalwood candle out of your desk, light it, and spend a few precious minutes inhaling the aroma. If you're out and about in the world, you can place a few drops of oil on a cotton ball and take it with you in a plastic bag to prepare for this twenty-minute vacation.

Pick a shaded location, perhaps in a park or near a lake or fountain. Even if the rest of the world is rushing by you, this is your time to develop a good rapport with the sense of peace that waits inside you to be liberated. Take the cotton ball and hold it between your palms so that your skin warms the cotton and brings out the aroma within. Cup your hands near your face, and inhale deeply and steadily, taking in the scent of the oil with the oxygen.

Think back to one time when you were blissfully happy, at peace with yourself and the world. Were you alone or with a companion? What time of year was it? How old were you? Take another deep breath, and conjure up the person you were then. Experience the effects of the essential oil wafting through you, filling you with a bright energy that smells as good as it feels.

Slowly open your eyes, and see the day in front of you. What can you change in yourself to make it more tolerable, to create a feeling of progress and ease? Exhale all the stale air and the tension inside, and with the next inhalation, get up, start walking, and enjoy the sense of relaxation that floods your mind and body.

20 ❧ Hand It to Your Feet

When you pamper your feet and hands, everything in between lets go of its tension. So, prepare for a delicious twenty minutes as you take care of yourself. By pressing various points on the foot, you can balance energy and enhance healing somewhere else in the body. All you need for this minivacation is a bottle of body lotion, or you can make this experience even more effective by using an aromatherapy oil with a calming effect such as neroli, bergamot, or ylang-ylang. Mix a few drops of the oil in an unscented lotion that you can buy in any drugstore.

Before you start your vacation, take off your shoes and socks. If you're wearing pantyhose, you can keep them on if you absolutely can't spare the time to change, but it's better to feel your bare toes.

Start with a basic hand massage. Your hands have to be relaxed so that they don't send the wrong message to your feet. Treat yourself to the luxury of touch. Take off your rings, watch, and bracelets, and pour a little lotion into the palm of one hand. Join the hands together, warming them and spreading the soft lotion to each digit of each finger. Make sure the backs of your hands are given appropriate attention. Do everything to these hands: rub them, pinch them lightly, knock the knuckles together, scratch them a little with your nails. See how alive the hands can be as they respond. It doesn't matter if they're a little chapped or even arthritic; as you work hand on hand, you'll start to feel the stiffness and pain melt away.

When your hands are nice and warm, shake them out from the wrists. Sit on the floor or on a couch, with your back well supported. Bend your knees, bring your feet in toward your trunk, and grasp them with both hands. Look at those feet! They are the workhorses of your body; they take you where you need to go. Since stress builds up calcium and lymph deposits in the feet, massaging them helps in a purely mechanical way: you can break up and reduce these sources of discomfort. Working on the feet also channels energy through your limbs, up your spine, and into your brain. After one of these vacations, you'll feel as if you could leap tall buildings at a single bound.

One hand will hold the foot steady while the other works on the various points. Let your thumb do most of the work, either pressing directly on a point, making a circle around the point, or gliding along. Your four fingers, meanwhile, will grip the toes, hold them back, and pull them forward. You may find, on this vacation, that you have never really looked at your feet or felt their various planes, angles, and curves before.

Close your eyes, and visualize your vacation spot: You are on a white sand beach that hugs a cobalt sea. There is a light breeze blowing, so the temperature feels perfect. You dip one foot into the sand, then the other. You are sitting beneath a palm tree, and you can smell wild grasses as you lean back and start to work on your feet with your hands.

Start with the tops of the feet, and work them with all your fingers. Do a general run-through: give the tops, bottoms, and sides a little preliminary attention. Then take one foot in both hands. Flex it, pulling the tops of the toes toward you. Extend your foot as far away from the body as it will go. Press your thumbs into the center above the arch, and point and flex the toes around the pressure. Change feet and repeat.

Draw your fingers down the length of the foot, run them along the tendons on the top, and then press the toes back toward the body. Interlace your fingers in your toes, and wiggle the toes back and forth and up and down. Make a fist, press it into the soles of each foot, and rub the knuckles on each area: heel, pad, arch, and ball. Slap the foot gently with your hands to stimulate the skin. Finally, cup each foot in both hands.

End your vacation by standing up again. See what it's like to have two new feet, revitalized by your calming touch. In just twenty minutes, you've learned the delight of what it means to take a load off.

21 ✷ Running Hot and Cold

Most of us are aware of a temperature that feels just right to us. We decide how much clothing to wear each day because of our inner thermometer. We also know how we shudder when suddenly hit with cold, and how we pull our hand away when something is scalding. These are self-protective reactions. They also say something about our anticipation of life's extremes. In order to shake up perceptions of what's hot and cold and in between, take this twenty-minute trip to a different set of sensations.

Begin with two pots or pans. Fill one with cold water and a few ice cubes, and fill the other with hot water from the tap. Be careful: if it's sending up a plume of steam, it's too hot. Start with your hands, since this is the part of your body most accustomed to feeling and sensing. Immerse your right hand in the cold water; your left goes in the hot. Sit quietly and become aware of the discrepancy in your two hands. Which one feels more mobile under the water? Which sensation do you prefer? Now quickly switch them. What happens when you put the cold hand into the hot water and the hot hand into the cold water? Take a minute for them to reach a new equilibrium. Finally, pull both hands out and examine them. Let the fingertips touch and exchange their drops of water. See how both cold and hot calm down and become room temperature as your own inner thermometer takes over.

Now refill the pans with hot and cold and do the exercise on your face. Again, make certain the hot water isn't scalding. Use two washcloths, letting one sit on your face until you have a clear impression of just what it feels like, before switching to the other. Cold, then hot, then cold, then hot. Do you find yourself wincing or gasping as you alternate cloths? What does this say about your ability to handle new situations? Keep at it until you can make the transition smoothly from one temperature to the other. Finally, apply both washcloths at the same time—one on each side of your face. You may start to find that your brain makes the accommodation for you and assimilates both temperatures so that they feel like one.

As you go through your day and find that it contains extremes that are hard to handle, remember this exercise, and recall that you have the ability to add a little cold to your hot and a little hot to your cold in order to make the experience warm and completely comfortable.

3
Desk Dreaming

Meaningless meetings, looming deadlines, hard-to-please bosses . . . you need something more than a quick lunch at your desk or a bit of gossip near the water cooler to relieve the anxiety of a day at the office. The ideas in this chapter will make the day seem much shorter and will give you the energy to fill the rest of your working hours productively.

22 ❧ A Dip in the Sea

When you're in your business clothes, it's hard to feel free and easy. A tie or high heels can take the relaxation out of the best vacationers, and even your dress-down clothes get stodgy after a while. Think for a minute: when do you most feel like yourself? When you're barefoot on the beach, getting sand between your toes. And that's where you're going on this vacation.

Wait a second!, you're probably saying, *that's impossible*. The uptight office is about as far from any beach as from the moon. But all you have to do is bring the beach to the office, and you're on top of the game. And when your colleagues on your team find out about this trip, they'll probably be swarming your office, trying to get in for a quick dip.

In order to bring the beach to the office, you need to go to a toy store and purchase a small bag of clean sandbox sand. You'll also need a container with a lid big enough for both your feet, which you can find at bed and bath stores. Pour a healthy amount of sand into your pan. When not in use, your beach-front property can be kept under your desk or tucked away beneath a bookcase in your office or cubicle.

When the boss is on your back and your project is limping along, take just twenty minutes for a beach break. It doesn't matter what season it is. As a matter of fact, it can be fun going to your office beach in the dead of winter when no one in his or her right mind would plan a trip to the shore.

It's time to leave the world of work. Take off your shoes and socks or stockings, and dip your feet into the cool, beckoning sand in your pan. Close your eyes, and feel the hot sun beat down on you. You can almost hear the pound of the surf, the waves breaking on the shore and then receding back into the ocean. Listen closely, and you'll hear the call of seagulls and the angry cry of kids when somebody inadvertently messes up their castle. You can smell the salt air, taste the hot dogs and fries, and hear the musicians tuning up in the bar across the boardwalk.

Be with the beach. Stretch out your feet, and scrunch them up in the sand. Rub the outsides, then the insides, and pretend you're taking a walk. Some of the sand may feel wet and damp, making it harder to pick up your feet and keep a good stride as you move along. Some of the sand may seem dry and delicate, ready to blow away in the first wind. And some of it may hide beautiful shells, which you can imagine as you reach down and grab a handful of sand.

Slowly, easily, you're going to end your vacation by dusting off your feet one at a time, placing them carefully back on the carpeting. Look at the great tan you got just sitting at your desk! Enjoy the sensation that your body had of being buffeted by the summer winds. Think about that cool shower that awaits you when you get to the cabana; think about a tall beer or a drink with an umbrella in it at the end of this long day.

If you're not relaxed by now, you never will be. And that vacation calls to you again and again, giving you just the boost you need when the day is bleak and summer seems far away.

23 ❋ Color Yourself Relaxed

If your desk is piled with papers, no one will spot the coloring book that you keep right next to your in-box. Here's a relaxing vacation that allows you to be creative and lazy, both at the same time.

So, you're not a great artist; that doesn't matter. You don't actually have to draw anything, which takes the pressure off. You probably haven't thought much about coloring since kindergarten, but if you'll give it a few minutes of nostalgic time, you may remember how much fun it was to lie on your stomach on a rainy day and fill in the shapes in your coloring book. Maybe the page was decorated with princesses and unicorns, or maybe it was trucks and cars. You had a huge box of 128 crayons with every color, from fuchsia to olive, and you could use them in any way you liked. And that's what you'll do now.

You'll want to visit a toy store or the kids' department of a bookstore and pick up a big paperback coloring book. The subject should be something you loved as a kid and still love today. Flip through the pages to get a sense of what's going on. Sometimes the book tells a complete story; sometimes it's just filled with images that conjure up different situations or emotions.

Don't think about staying in the lines or working from page to page—that's kid stuff! You want to use this vacation creatively, making the juxtaposition of color the chief element. Try people with tawny faces and crimson eyes, trees with peach leaves or cobalt trunks. Who cares whether the colors match or even complement each other? Of course, if your goal is to make a truly harmonious, elegant painting, you can do that, too. This is your game, and you can play it any way you want.

Use the crayons delicately, shading things with a light hand, or let your determination come to the surface as you scrub away with a black pencil, hard, making the outlines sharp and angular. Try coloring with your nonprimary hand. Although it will feel awkward, you may get results you never dreamed of. You can easily take up twenty minutes letting your hand wander the page, doing exactly what it wants.

If you like, hang your favorite piece for all to see. Enjoy the freedom of scrawling and stippling as you will. This is a voyage that brings out the creative side of you.

24 ❖ Pumping Office Iron

You can go to the gym after work, but why not take a break from the daily routine and work out right in your office? Studies on the best uses of the workplace have shown that people who take active breaks throughout the day, who stretch out cramped muscles and get oxygen moving through their bodies, are far more productive than the grinds who sit enslaved to their computers hour after hour.

So, take twenty minutes once a day if you can to jump around and move. You have a great choice of activities for a six-by-six-foot office or cubicle and you may even choose to do more than one (cross training) on each vacation.

Hand Weights

You don't have to bench-press 200 pounds to feel the burn. Start with small weights. You can purchase five-pound hand weights, or use two paperweights or dictionaries to do arm lifts (great work to stave off arthritis or carpal tunnel, two common office maladies). If you aren't sure you want to invest in weights, start off with two bags of sugar encased in plastic bags with handles. Stand up, and swing your arms back and forth. Lift and lower them, being careful to keep your elbows pointing down and not to lift your shoulders. Hold the weights just below shoulder height for a count of ten, then slowly lower them. Be sure to keep breathing as you do your weights.

Dynabands

These elasticized bands, with handles on either end, come in different colors, indicating how hard or easy they are to pull. But you don't need designer bands to enjoy the stretch. You can simply use an old inner tube from a bicycle tire, available (usually for free) at your local bike store. The band should measure from the floor to your shoulder when extended. You can roll your band up and stash it in a corner of your bookcase when not in use.

Start this part of your vacation by stretching the band out. Pull evenly with each hand, and feel the dynamic tension. Now let your body move. Bring the band up over your head, and lean to the right, then to the left. Put the handles on the floor, and anchor the band with your feet, then take the middle of the band with both hands and do pull-ups (bend your elbows, and pull both hands in toward your chest).

You can go wild with this tool. For a good twist, wrap it around your waist, and pull on one side, then the other. Or hook it around your doorknob, hold on with both hands, and lean back on your heels. Just make sure the boss isn't about to open your door while you're working out!

Yoga

One of the oldest and most beneficial types of exercise is the Indian practice of yoga, derived from the word for "yoke" or "union." Yoga consists of many different postures that stretch the body and improve the spirit. You can hold postures for any length of time—as you breathe into each one, you discover that it becomes slightly easier to get deeper into the posture.

One particularly nice exercise to do in the office is the "tree" because it teaches balance, something sorely lacking in most office situations. Take off your shoes and socks. Stand with your feet together, and slowly shift so that you have 100 percent of your weight on one foot. Slide the unweighted foot up the side of the opposite leg until it comes to rest wherever you are comfortable. If you are very flexible and have excellent balance, it will sit high on your thigh; if you're just starting out with this posture, it may sit just above the ankle on the side of the calf. Place your hands in front of your chest in a prayer posture, and slowly lift them until they come to rest directly over the crown of your head. Now switch sides. Breathe into the posture; don't worry if you waver or stagger. Come out of it, and come back into it. The longer you hold it, the more relaxed you'll be.

Tai Chi

Tai chi chuan, an ancient Chinese form of exercise and meditation, is similar to yoga in that it unifies and balances the body, mind, and spirit. Unlike yoga, tai chi is always moving, although slowly. One posture melts imperceptibly into the next.

Try this one as you walk barefoot across your office: hold an imaginary ball in front of your solar plexus, and with all your weight on your right foot, turn the ball and draw it down toward your right. Step with your left foot, and lift the ball up, then twist at the waist, and move the ball down to your left as you step left. With all the weight on your left leg, lift the ball, twist at the waist, then move the ball down to your right as you step right. Continue across the room, inhaling as you draw the ball up, exhaling as you place the ball down.

These various office activities will keep you alert and alive through those dull days. Physical exercise offers a whole new perspective for your mind.

25 ❧ *Feng Shui* Getaway

The Chinese believe that there is an art and a science to creating balance and harmony in our personal spaces. This consideration of how we use our environment is called *feng shui*, or "the way of wind and water," or the natural forces of the universe. The theory of this ancient practice, also known as geomancy, is that all the things in your life have their own energy, and by arranging them in a certain way, you can make that energy move in a positive rather than a negative direction. With good *feng shui*, wealth and abundance can flow, mental and emotional attitudes can improve, and in some cases, illness vanishes.

In the purely functional environment of most offices, you have ample room to change elements and add others. Objects should be evenly balanced within a space, and as much as possible, natural elements should be included. This is easy to do in an office, where a plant, a dangling crystal pendant, or a goldfish bowl may turn the tide toward good *feng shui*.

In China professionals are called in for architectural consultations so that no building is ever designed without these factors in mind. A design should take in the five elements—wood, fire, earth, metal, and water—and the eight sides that represent a form known as the *bagua*. These sides begin at the front door, representing career, while the back of the house or room represents fame. The left center is family and health; the right center is children and inspiration. The upper left is wealth; the upper right is partnership or marriage. The lower left is helpful people and travel, and the lower right is knowledge and accumulated wisdom. The spot of power is wherever you spend most of your time. In your office, that would most likely be your desk.

According to *feng shui* theory, the juxtaposition of different elements in a house or office is the deciding factor in the success or failure of a venture.

On this vacation, you are going to assess your office for maximum energy and make just a few changes that will enhance what you've already got. Do you think your office has the right design? First, look at your desk. It should face the door so that you can see who's coming in. The thinking behind this is that you don't want to be surprised. It's never a good idea to let anyone sneak up on you, and you'll be much calmer if you feel in control of the situation. So, you might like to spend your time (with a little help, of course) turning your desk in the correct direction. If this is impossible—if it's bolted to the floor, or there are built-in units in every other area—you'll have to use a "cure." In this case, you can cure a bad situation simply by hanging a mirror. This way, you can glance into it when someone approaches and see who's behind you.

In addition, you want to be certain that whatever it is that makes you successful has the most opportune position in your office. For example, if a computer drives your work, it should be in the wealth area. In order to maximize its potential, hang a multifaceted leaded crystal charm in that area of the office.

When sunlight hits the crystal, you get a beautifully colored rainbow exactly where you need to get energy moving. Same goes for an artist's drawing board or a cook's preparation area.

If you have a few minutes left after you've moved your desk and hung your plant or crystal, get rid of clutter. If you have a file cabinet that's crammed with old papers that you never use, weed them out. Look around and see whether you have certain items that haven't been moved in a year. If you need them, pick them up and put them somewhere else in the office. You will be astounded at how these small changes will start to make a big difference in your life.

Remember the old Chinese proverb: "If there is harmony in the house, there is order in the nation. If there is order in the nation, there will be peace in the world." What a rewarding twenty minutes you've just spent!

26 ✹ Get the Ball Rolling

You've been clicking that mouse all day, typing up a storm, filing when you aren't busy with meetings. Your hands and fingers are so cramped that you can barely pick up your coffee cup.

So, on this vacation, you're going to pamper those hands and exercise them lovingly. You'll need a pair of golf balls (which you can get in any sporting goods store) or Chinese exercise balls (available in martial arts stores and through many stress-relief catalogs).

Hold one ball in each hand, and feel their weight. Roll them from the center of your palm to the fingers, then back again. (Chinese exercise balls are hollow, with a sounding plate inside, one ball pitched high and the other low; as you twist them in your hands, you make a lovely melody.) Does one hand ache more than the other? Usually your primary hand takes the brunt of the work. Close your eyes for a minute, and imagine the tension running out of your hands, into the balls, and then out into the air. Open your hands flat, balancing the balls, then curl your fingers and wrist in toward your body. Open and close several times, working the wrists back and forth. Now extend the hands out, flexing the wrists, as though you were going to let the balls roll off your fingertips (cup the fingers inward so that this doesn't happen). Bring them back into your palm.

Now hold both balls in your primary hand. Using your thumb and fingers, manipulate them so that they turn in circles, rolling in and out from your thumb and fingers to your palm.

Switch to your nonprimary hand. You may feel that you're nowhere near as dexterous with this one, but if you go more slowly, you can usually make a few circuits.

Now balance one ball between your pinky and fourth finger and balance the other between your index and third fingers. Without using your thumb, switch the balls, easing them down toward the palm, then into the other set of fingers. Now try walking the ball from one set of fingers to the next—pinky and ring finger to ring finger and third finger, to third finger and index, to index and thumb—and then back again. Switch hands.

You'll probably drop the balls a good deal on this vacation, but so what? As those balls roll off your palms, your stress rolls off your mind—and you'll end up feeling great.

27 ❧ Tunes to Tame Your Tension

A great beat can drive away the blues, but how can you listen to your tunes when the whole office is busy at work like bees in a hive? The answer, of course, is that you can turn up the sound as loud as you want on your Walkman (just watch those decibels on your eardrums).

When you're in the world of sound, nothing else penetrates. You don't have to think about the project due or the roar of your boss chewing out another employee. You don't have to concern yourself with other people's emotions or lack of them. The gang at the water cooler vanishes, and you are left alone, onstage. You are the show now—you are the star.

If you have a door, close it so that you can slip off your shoes and play air guitar or dance to the pounding beat. If you're in a cubicle, or your space is too cramped for dancing, you'll have to content yourself with tapping your feet, but be sure you do that. Get up and sway to the music. Get that beat in your bones, your muscles, even your eyelashes.

The rhythm of any piece of music gets us back on track. The reason may have something to do with our instinctive response to the heartbeat we heard when we were inside our mothers, before we knew the world and how difficult it could be. When you start grooving to the basic one-and-a-two-and-a-three-and-a-four, you have a built-in regulator to help adjust your mood.

Follow the bass line of the song. That great rhythmic vibration shakes your whole body and wakes you up to a new way of seeing life. When you're feeling depressed or kind of out of it, this type of intensity is the best tonic you could ask for. The wash of music over your soul is curative: it does a lot more than soothe a savage breast. Sometimes you may want a quiet, reflective piece, and jazz is good for that. Or maybe you can't deal with another human being, so you turn on the blues. Classical is great for getting organized; rock for when you just want to howl. You can get down with a rapper, or sob a country tune all about losing your job, your lover, and your dog.

Really listen to the music; don't use it as background noise. Follow its patterns and phrases, and think about a scene that it calls to mind for you. Bring yourself into the picture, and see if you can't use the sound around you to resolve some of the tension you feel.

When it's time for the piece to end, sit for a minute and get yourself together before taking off your headphones and returning to the world of work. This trip is a real escape from reality, one that you can take again and again.

28 ❧ Hoop Dreams

So, you're ready to scrap this job and try out for the NBA? Fuhgedabowdit. You're probably not tall enough and your aim is not exactly on the mark every single time. Shaquille O'Neil would not consider you a threat.

Still, there's no reason you can't dream. Why not put a hoop in your office and dunk some basketballs when the going gets rough? A suction-cup hoop with a miniature styrofoam ball is usually available in office supply stores, although in a pinch, you can use your wastebasket and a wadded-up piece of paper.

Office basketball is an essential vacation. It gives you the opportunity to practice hand-eye coordination and perfects the accuracy of your aim. Of course, it also provides the satisfaction of scoring. This is important not only for basketball buffs—anyone can use the benefits of this game in real life. Why else do you think they came up with expressions such as "What are you aiming for?" and "Keep your eye on the ball"? Getting to your creative and financial goals may be quite similar to dunking a basket.

Use your chair on wheels to simulate scooting around the court. Your office is probably carpeted, and that will slow you down, but it may also have one of those hard plastic carpet-protectors that let you move like the wind. A shot from just under the basket, on either side, or right in front scores two points. A long shot from all the way across the office wins you three points. You can pop out of your seat for extra momentum—but no hanging on the rim!

If you want a greater challenge, ask a buddy to bring his or her chair into your office and play one-on-one. Defense has to scoot more carefully to get access to the basket in order to shoot; offense is going to try to zoom in between the opponent and the basket. Chair basketball is safe—it's difficult to get injured in this game—and twenty minutes of it will distract you from whatever problems you may be having. Playing like this is also a good way to open up avenues of communication with colleagues. If you can be civil on the court, you can deal with each other in business, too. Just be careful you don't get fouled-out from traveling with the ball.

There's excitement in the air when the clock is running down and that big meeting looms in just a few minutes. Quick—shoot! Not quite in—try again! The agony and ecstasy of office hoop ball offers you a trip you won't soon forget.

29 ✸ On-Line Adventures

It's just human nature—we all love gossip. We like to talk about other people because, well, it makes us feel that we're in the know. Also, we love to think that we have the scoop on someone, especially if the gossip is juicy. But be warned: it's always safer to gossip with people you don't know. It saves a lot of hurt feelings, and at the office, it could save your job!

The Internet provides a wonderful forum for reading up on delicious gossip that is completely safe. What's best, you never have to reveal where you got your information. So, take a break when the work pressure is building up, and go on-line to read those fabulous tidbits. (Since your organization probably frowns on a lot of time on-line for non-work-related tasks, you'll want to avoid chat-rooms; instead, enjoy a quick read through the gossip pages.)

It's like being a fly on the wall. The things that people gossip about—celebrities, politicians, who's doing what with whom, what the latest trend or fad is—are a respite from the serious matters that take up most of your day.

For a twenty-minute on-line vacation, pick something you love to talk about and find an appropriate message board. Then listen to what others are saying. (You'll be able to repeat all this information later at the water cooler.) The neat thing about reading the gossip pages is that you don't have to get involved. You can just sit back and enjoy the ride. When your time is up, log off, and take a few minutes to relish the vicarious experience of knowing the intimate details of other people's lives—and probably their vacations, too!

30 ✻ Thanks for the Memories

When you're caught up in office politics and deadlines, it's hard to remember all the things that make life worthwhile. It's a lot more than a paycheck or a boost up the career ladder, although those are important. And while a major reason for being at work in the first place is to make things nicer for the family you love, it's even more than that.

There are people in your life who have left a mark, even if it's not one that's readily apparent. You don't have to see these friends on a regular basis to recall exactly what it was about them—their sense of humor, their quiet wisdom, or their never-failing ability to see through your ploys or excuses—that made them crucial in your life. The gratitude you feel toward them is probably reciprocated, and what better way to express it but to let them know?

Take a vacation from work, and sit down and write them a letter. Not an e-mail message, to be tossed off in the blink of an eye, but a real, old-fashioned letter. Don't write it on company stationery; instead, pick out a nice creamy stock from an office supply store, complete with matching envelope. If you're into antiques, or you just love the feel of a good writing implement, invest in a fountain pen, the modern ones that take cartridges— you don't even get ink on your fingers.

Sit down with your paper and pen, and think for a minute before you start writing. What do you want to say? How do you want to say it? In a phone call, you'd probably stammer out the basics—*how are you? how's the job? how's the kids?* Those routine questions usually fall from our lips because we're not sure we have anything else to say.

But when you have the luxury of twenty minutes to write, you can get past the niceties. You can reminisce about the old times, ask questions about your pal's current life, and launch into a description of what you're doing, who you hang out with, and maybe even what you dream about for the future. Once you get rolling, it's often hard to stop. You can be funny or serious or both. If you simply can't bear to get down deep, you can just talk about last night's Knicks game the way you used to when you were in high school together. Don't waste time griping and complaining; instead, find something that you haven't been able to confide in anyone else. It's sometimes surprising how you can just fall back into your old patterns of communicating, even when you haven't been in touch. That's the wonderful thing about friendships: they last because whatever it is about them that's important gets internalized. You have forgotten whatever friction came between you and are washed with lovable memories. The way that the two of you learned to give and take never goes away, and that's something to be very grateful for.

It's also a good thing, when you haven't seen a friend in a while, to have the framework of written correspondence between you. When you don't have to think about those extra five pounds you gained or the gray in your hair, you can concentrate on what's vital.

The other person will probably be astounded that you wrote—and rather flattered, as well. And if you're really in sync, that friend will just be picking up a pen to write you when your missive arrives in the mail.

4

The Great Outdoors

The birds are singing, the wind blows in your hair, and the smell of grass tickles your nose. Here are twenty-minute adventures outside your own four walls to help you let go and feel at peace with nature.

31 ❧ April Showers

In April, one of the loveliest things you can do for yourself is to take a walk in the rain. The change of seasons used to be a powerful force in our lives. As the ice and snow of winter melted away, people could rejoice in the return of warm sunshine that would allow them to peel off their heavy layers of clothing and plant crops. Today, of course, we barely notice the spring equinox because we're locked inside offices with windows that don't open, and we per-ambulate from job to home to the market and to our kids' lacrosse practice inside a car with processed air. We may never really get to delight in the fresh, clean scent of the first days of spring.

Pick a time of day that you particularly like, dress appropriately for the weather, and go for it. If you live in a city, get yourself to a park or a waterfront area and start from there. If you live in the suburbs, drive to a more remote area, where the traffic won't disturb your idyll. If you already live in the country, take advantage of the deep woods at this time of year. Be careful not to skip anything. See whether the trees are housing any nests; look down and see the tracks of raccoon, possums, or deer. See if the cloud patterns in the sky betray any hint of lazy summer thunderstorms. What does the rain feel like on your face? On your hands? If you stand quietly and listen, what other sounds can you pick up that reverberate through the quiet?

There is always something new to notice: the thick odor of decaying leaves and branches, the flight of tiny birds flushed out of a tree by a roaming squirrel, a rabbit hopping across a patch of untouched spring snow.

And speaking of early-spring snow, it's a great omen if you find it. If you should discover a patch of white on the ground in April, you're in luck: washing your face in early-spring snow is said to keep you wrinkle-free for life.

When you're out in a field or in a forest, you will smell, hear, see, and feel all sorts of new life starting up. If you go out in the morning, there will be robins plucking worms from the ground, mourning doves cooing calmly in the shelter of trees, blue jays starting their nests. You will see the muddy stirrings of life under the soil: crocuses and snowdrops peeking up; daffodil and tulip leaves just rimming the grass. And the grass itself, long brown and yellow from winter's devastation, will start to show signs of green again.

You will feel the fine mist of drops on your face. But unlike the chilling, breath-holding pelting of a winter rain, this experience gives you the feeling that you've been washed clean. Don't duck your head to avoid the drops—go ahead and lift your face to the sky for the full treatment. For the more adventuresome: take off your shoes and feel the wet grass and soft earth between your toes.

It's the aromas that will give you the feeling that you're on vacation. You will smell the heady scent of the soil and, if you're lucky, the various herbs and shrubs that have a distinctive odor and are just beginning to fight their way back from their quiet sleep of many months. If you are near a pine forest, the wet needles will give off their perfume; if you walk past a house with a fireplace, you'll sniff the warm logs as they burn and crackle through the chimney. Someone may have indulged in a first mow, and the cut grass will smell sweet enough to eat. If you happen to be near the sea, you can stomp through hard-packed sand and enjoy the salt spray on your face.

Walk slowly. Keep your wits about you. Make your senses pay attention.

32 ✻ The Art of Swing

I'll just bet that every time you pass a playground, you have an unquenchable desire to jump right in and act like a kid. Sure, you feel silly, but that's ok. Remember what it used to be like? You whizzing down the slide; you sitting down hard on the seesaw so your friend went squealing into the stratosphere, begging you to let him down; you swinging higher with every stroke, nearly touching the trees with your toes.

Well, playgrounds have changed a lot, and they're even more fun than they used to be. For a twenty-minute break, this is one of the most rewarding junkets you can manage.

First, of course, you have to consider when you're going to use the equipment. You will probably feel too self-conscious acting like a kid when there are other kids present. If the nearest playground to you is in an elementary school, you probably won't be allowed on the premises during school hours (too bad, because the equipment is just sitting there, abandoned and lonely while the kids are locked up in classrooms). But after school and in the evening, the place is up for grabs. And if you live near a park with a playground, you'll have even more flexibility. No one's going to throw you out; you just have to work up the gumption to use it.

So, now that you're here, what should you do first? Start with the basics. Swinging, in particular, is a great stress reliever. The simple, hypnotic motion will relax you, and the air rushing past you will feel wonderfully refreshing.

Then there's the slide. There are all sorts of slides now: you can come down straight, or you can twist and turn on your way. The exhilaration you feel sitting up at the top, your legs dangling in front of you, your body higher than anyone else's in the playground, is rarely matched. The nice thing about sliding is that you feel out of control, but you really have a lot of control. Even the new editions, featuring a slide in the shape of a corkscrew, look a lot more formidable than they actually are. And if you want proof that you're the one in charge, you can simply walk up from the bottom. When you get the knack, you'll find that you enjoy coming down on your stomach as much as on your bottom. You can even lie back and pretend you're an astronaut, training for a new mission. Just slide, and your feet will find the ground by themselves.

And there's more! Today's playgrounds have ropes to climb, tires to swing on, barrels through which you can grope your way. They have elaborate agility steps—a cluster of plastic mushrooms at different heights that allow you to practice falling and not falling as you make your way (carefully) around the circle.

This is just like real life. Finding balance is a constant quest. As soon as we think we've got it, everything shifts, and we have to start over again.

Next, there are nets worthy of a pirate's frigate that will take you up to the top of a lookout tower. And replacing the monkey bars of old are the nontoxic, nonrustable handholds that will produce, over time, a couple of beautifully developed biceps. You, too, can be a monkey, swinging from tree to tree.

Taking a twenty-minute vacation in a playground allows you to set your own limits, take a few risks, and shout with joy when you figure out the right combination of elements.

33 ❋ Sounding Off

When you were little, one of the best things to do was make a lot of noise over a long period of time. Your mother would take you by the shoulders and promptly direct you out the door. "Go scream at a tree" she might have said to you.

But then all you had to do was get together with a couple of friends, and the noise level escalated. When you played, you'd go all out, laughing, hooting, growling, and hollering. No one could shut you up because outside was the place to be loud. You weren't interrupting anyone's conversation; you weren't disturbing anyone who wanted to sleep or watch tv. When you got older, you could go to a game and cheer till you were blue in the face for your team. You might also have gone to a rock concert and screamed along with the mob.

It was a wonderful release. You could get out all the frustration, boredom, anger, joy, and pain that you usually kept bottled up inside. Yelling was great therapy.

It still is, but it's a little more awkward to leave the house and start screaming. When you're a grown-up, you need a little cover. You're going to have to find a place where you can be completely alone. A beach at sunrise or a park at sunset is a perfect location.

Sit on the grass and let things bubble up inside you. You want to sense the rumble of something big deep down in your gut, like a whale about to emerge from the ocean. You are going to match the power and ear-splitting sound of a train or plane with your own lungs.

You may be out of practice when it comes to being loud. I wouldn't advise you to jump into sound without preparation; that way lies a couple of aching vocal chords and a case of laryngitis. Before you throw yourself into the experience, you'll need a little practice creating sound from deep in your belly.

Begin with a few deep breaths so that you can expand and contract your stomach muscles. Pump the air in and out of your center like a bellows. Now let some sound come out with it. Don't think about shouting; think about erupting like a volcano. You are bubbling up from underneath; you are a sleeping giant just awakened. You are now ready to match any locomotive note for note.

Stand up, and spread your legs apart to give yourself a good physical base. You are a train. Imagine it in your mind. You are fast, moving in a straight line, building up speed, charging down the track. You can feel the moment approaching, feel the power mounting inside you to explode. Every other noise will fade away. The honk of cars will fade into the distance; the sound of squealing brakes or light machinery are as nothing compared with you. You are the biggest, the loudest—no contest.

Think about whatever it is that you've been longing to release. Is there someone you'd like to curse out? Are you fed up with your boss's demands? Have you never yelled at your kids for fear of traumatizing them? Do you hold back when you have an argument with your significant other?

This is the time to let them all have it. You are VERY VERY
LOUD. Let it come up from your roots, from your deepest emotions. Now! SCREAM! YELL! Make a huge noise!

When it's all over, you'll be panting hard, and your heart
will be beating wildly. You will have experienced a cathartic
release that can carry you for days. This is a powerful vacation,
not one to start with. But after you've done it once, watch out—
you may become addicted to making noise.

34 ✷ Rock Heavy, Rock Light

This vacation will take your mind somewhere it has never been.
We all know that the mind is powerful, but when you embark
on this particular journey, you will be confounded and myste-
riously pleased to find that your mind can do anything it
decides to do. Including change the weight of two rocks.

First, you must find some perfect rocks. They should fit
nicely in the palm of your hand, and they can be beautiful or
unremarkable. It's a good idea to start out with two of almost
equal size, although if you enjoy this vacation and take it on a
regular basis, you'll find that it doesn't much matter how similar or dissimilar your rocks are.

Sit down somewhere comfortable, and look at your chosen
specimens. Examine the different planes, the texture of the
stone, the colors that underlie or highlight the rocks. If they've
been washed by water, they will have at least one side that's
totally smooth. Some rocks are flattened ovals of sheer, hard
perfection; others are jagged and irregular. You can heft them in
one hand together, then separate them and enjoy the contrast
between the ungiving rock and your porous skin.

Did I say *ungiving*? Of course, I meant only in terms of its
composition. Rocks are actually catalysts for imaginative specu-
lation. (Where did this hard gray thing come from? How did it

get here? How old is it? Did it break off from a bigger rock? How long might it last before being shattered to smithereens in a rock slide?) The basic question to ask, however, is: What do these rocks have to do with me, and with my vacation?

Taking one rock in each hand, close your eyes. Open and close your hands lightly around the rocks, sensing their place in your palms. You may wish to rest the backs of your hands on your knees. Now open your hands, and just be still. Concentrate on the feeling of rock on skin.

Also concentrate on the weight of the rock in each hand. Even if you've consciously picked two stones that seem to balance each other out, if you sit for a few minutes, you will discover that one is heavier than the other. It will feel bigger in your hand.

Think, first, about the heavier rock. Imagine it growing out of your hand, pulling it down. Think only about this one stone in this one hand. Nothing else has any importance right now. If your thoughts drift from the weight of this rock, gently guide them back.

After you've spent perhaps three or four minutes contemplating the heavier stone, turn your attention to your other hand. This rock should seem like a pebble, so light that it almost wants to levitate from your palm. You can bring your mind right to this delicate fragment and away from everything else. The rock is so insubstantial that you may have to secure it with one finger, just to make sure it doesn't float away. It seems as though a butterfly had just landed in your hand.

Now compare the two rocks at once, allowing your mind to vacillate from one hand to the other. *Heavy, light; heavy, light.*

Your mind is now going to perform the alchemy I mentioned earlier. Still with eyes closed, take a breath, and let your mind return to the first hand, the one with the heavy rock. You will start to notice how the rock is changing in your hand, how the pressure of it is lifting off your palm, and how it is slowly becoming a mere shadow of its former self. As a matter of fact, this once ponderous piece is now barely noticeable. It is so light that it may just fly up in your face and you would hardly notice it, as though a speck of dust had glanced off of you.

And that second hand, the hand with the tiny, delicate, light rock: as you switch your mind back to think about this rock, you will notice that it is gaining weight, as though it had just eaten a huge meal or been drenched in a cement bath. As you hold it, your hand is beginning to ache. You can't believe that this thing actually fits in your palm. At this rate, as it grows, it seems to be turning into a boulder. The heavy rock has become light; the light rock has become heavy.

Open your eyes slowly, and look at the two rocks in your hand. They are the very ones you started out with, but now you can see their potential. They are anything you want them to be. And they can remind you of other things in your life that seem fixed and immutable but can, with a little willpower, change radically. What about this day? If it started out not so great, maybe you can turn it around. This also applies to a relationship you may have with someone, or to the dark and light sides of your own personality. They are all just as flexible and elastic as the two stones. And if you have the time to extend your vacation a little, go back to the beginning and switch the rocks again. Your mind will never tire of this amazing play.

35 ❋ Snowtime, Throwtime

On a perfect winter's day, you will feel the nip of snow in the air. There's a fresh, clean feeling to it, an awareness that the sky has changed and something's coming. Sometimes a snowfall begins imperceptibly, just a flake or two hitting your window, but sometimes it comes on with a fury, as though a few technicians up there were dumping out the contents of innumerable frozen pillows. The flakes get wet and soggy, and they are so white that they almost seem blue. First, the ground has a slight dusting, then the trees and porches and steps, and finally, you can barely see your hand in front of you. It's a genuine snow event!

You want to take advantage of the snow when it first arrives, before it becomes prey to roving plows and dogs and the dirt that settles down from days of tromping feet. At such times, the best use of nature's gift may be a snowball fight.

You need a pristine, just-fallen snow for perfect snowballs. The finest snow for packing is wet and heavy, although you can still have a respectable battle with dry, dusty flakes.

Spontaneity is a wonderful thing, so you may simply want to plunge into your snowball fight without any preparation as soon as you are overwhelmed with the inclination. On the other hand, most generals go into war with a battle plan, and they dress for the occasion. If you take the time to put on some protective gear, you can go back to whatever you were doing without shifting too many other gears after your twenty-minute campaign. This means you'll bundle up, put on boots and a parka, and wear mittens, which tend to keep your hands warmer than gloves.

If you're a competitive person, you may require a target that's human and moving. Make sure you enlist a friend who's up for the challenge. It is *de rigueur* to inform your opponents that they are about to be pelted . . . well, those are the strict rules of war, but who needs rules when you've got snowballs? Some of the best fun comes from surprise attacks. Of course, if you just want to get out there and let off some steam, then trees, cars, fire hydrants, and your own house or garage will do.

Snowball throwing is a multitasked activity that takes both coordination and speed. It's more complicated than slinging water balloons, for example, for which you prepare all your missiles in advance so you don't continually need to stop to make new ones. Or if you're having an autumn-leaf skirmish, you simply shove your opponent into piles of leaves. But with snowball fights, you have to do it all at once: you have to make your ammunition in the midst of battle. This vacation, thus, is not for the fainthearted, and may take some practice. Field tip: if you have the time, do make a set of snowballs (maybe eight or ten) before you start throwing. This way, you can work up momentum and not have to stop for supplies.

In order to test the quality and quantity of the snow, run your hands along a picket fence or a car roof, just to get the feel of the nice cold stuff. If all you've got is small, dry powder, you may have to create the impression of a lot of snow by gathering it all in with both arms and then shooing or splashing it on your victim (who should be close by to get the required effect).

Hopefully, however, you will have a nice dense, thick snow to work with. When you do, start by scooping up a handful and packing it tight, then adding to it, packing it down again. You don't want it too hard, especially if other people are going to be the recipients of your throw, but you need it solid enough to make a respectable projectile. Keep shaping lightly until the snow forms into a ball—not an oblong or a disk. Don't press down too hard, or your snow will turn to ice or, worse, to slush.

The best-size snowballs fit well in the palm of your hand with your fingers slightly open. However, if you're getting bombarded yourself while you're in production, you will not have time for this level of precision. You can fire off smaller shots if you don't have the luxury to refine your design, but bigger ones have more oomph.

Receiving snowballs is an art in itself. You have to turn, dodge, deflect, and, whenever possible, move aside so that the snow whams nicely into a tree, a house, or the ground and misses you completely. Your goal is not to be there when the snowball arrives. (Try to time your bending over to pick up new snow with your opponent's launch.) If you get hit, don't worry about it; if you let it annoy or frustrate you, your own snowball creation will suffer. Shake it off, and reload!

After twenty minutes of this winter fun, you will be exhausted, red-cheeked, and merry, ready to face the rest of the day with visions of snowballs dancing in your head.

36 ❦ It's All in the Wrist

Horseshoes have been around since, well, since horses started carrying humans around. And since you have to change a horse's shoes about every six weeks, there are always plenty of discarded shoes. The sets of four shoes and a post are sold in sporting goods stores, but if you happen to live near a stable, you can ask if they have any that you can take away.

Paint two shoes red and two blue (or yellow and green—who cares?). You can make stakes out of 3/4-inch metal pipes cut into two equal parts. Sharpen one end so that it will stick in the soil. Set your post in the ground with about a foot or a foot and a half sticking out. Walk away about thirty-five or forty feet, and you're good to go. A ringer (the horseshoe hugging the post) is three points; a leaner (the horseshoe touches the post) is two points, and you get one point for getting as close to the post as the open end of the shoe (about six inches, or the breadth of a man's hand).

Frankly, points don't matter. What really matters is the *clang!* of metal on metal. It's like shooting baskets, hitting the bull's-eye, or wasting those space invaders on the video games, except when you pitch horseshoes, you get an auditory as well as a visual kick. And of course, you have the breeze to contend with—working either with you or against you—and the good smell of the grass that you churn up underfoot.

If you play with someone else, you each take one color, and whoever gets twenty-one points first wins. But you also get to talk, to dish, to rib the other person, to walk around the post measuring one shoe as opposed to another. You get to compare and contrast the technique of your friend with your own.

Horseshoes has traditionally been a "guy" thing, like darts, pool, or bocce, but there's no reason that it should be gender specific. Women will find that the easy swing of a horseshoe is a relaxing way to test hand-eye coordination, to pit themselves against their own last score, and to just haul off and throw something that won't break.

And, as everyone knows, horseshoes bring good luck. If you throw really well, and the shoe happens to land with its two ends pointing toward the sky, your luck won't drain out, but will suffuse the rest of your day with a great feeling.

37 ❋ Chillin' in the City

Most of the time it's gritty and dirty, loud and irritating. The car fumes get in your eyes, and the sound of cabdrivers screaming at each other isn't conducive to relaxation. But if you wait until things quiet down, late at night, you'll find a wonderful vacation in store for you in the city.

If you have a dog, you probably already know the pleasures of the city at night. If you don't, this is a great time to get started. You'll want to wait until the late news is over. Most regular citizens are already in their jammies and slippers, and, toothbrush in hand, they are yawning their way toward bed.

You, on the other hand, are going on an adventure. In the dead of winter, you'll need some warm underwear, a turtleneck, a sweater and parka, some warm socks, warm gloves, boots, and a hat. More than twenty minutes out there, you'll need a bala-clava too (one of those face protectors that make you look like

a mugger), but you can always pull your scarf up in front of
your face. In mild weather, wear light clothing that makes you
easy to spot in the dark.

Naturally, you want to stay safe, so avoid parks and dark
streets. But the rest of the city is open territory. If your own
neighborhood isn't exactly hopping, then go where the lights are
brightest.

Walk briskly, but don't hurry at all. There are things you'll
see at night that you wouldn't see at any other time. Do a little
window-shopping in the closed-up stores; look up at apartment
windows for some visual eavesdropping. You may see couples
fighting, embracing, a lone cat staring at the moon, or a woman
crocheting by lamplight.

Catch the whiff of the air: it should be sharp and clean now
that the traffic has died down. You can see your breath in front
of you, and the moon overhead, leading you onward. The city
at night is a magical place, nothing at all like its daytime cousin.
Enjoy the variety of it, the grittiness as well as the surprising
friendliness of people. Look carefully at buildings, at the glint of
streetlights on windows, at the faces of people hurrying by or
loitering on corners. In cities late at night, people who are out
tend to be the more interesting ones, those who aren't afraid of
the dark and who have things to do long after the rest of the
world has gone to bed.

Stop into a twenty-four-hour diner or, even better, to a coffee shop where a few throwbacks to the beat generation read
poetry and play bad guitar. Warm up a little with a cup of joe.
You never know what interesting people you might encounter;
they are all companion travelers on your journey.

At last, this is a time for you to stake new claims to the
streets you know so well. Go back out into the night and stand
for a moment under a street lamp, letting the pool of light sur-
round and protect you. Look up at the silent, majestic buildings

right in front of you and feel like them—empowered to take
back the night.

38 ❋ Catch Spring Fever

Here's something you haven't done in years: roll down a hill.
Make it a long hill, with a majestic sweep of grass that goes on
and on. Do you remember being a kid and stretching out, holding your legs tight together and linking your hands overhead?
Just that position was enough to give you a rush unequal to any
you got on a roller coaster or Ferris wheel.

First, you must find the perfect hill. You're looking for a
gentle slope, one that starts off nearly flat but gets steeper as you
go. You want to pick up momentum on the way and then taper
off gradually as you slow down and finally stop. There can't be
anything in the way (such as a tree) or anything at the end of it
(such as a busy street or a fence) that would send you on a
detour from your truly fun vacation and give you welts and
bruises. The best hills are in big parks, with plenty of open
space around them.

You'll probably feel self-conscious at first because adults just
don't do things like this. But once you get going, you'll be moving too fast for anyone to spot you, and from a distance, you'll
look like a tall kid. Don't worry about it. Put your mind in the
roll, and who cares what people say? This is your private time,
and you can do whatever you like with it.

You'll want to feel light and airy during this vacation, so
choose a time when you haven't just eaten or feel full. If you're
wearing glasses take them off and put them in a safe place. Now
lie down on the grass, and just get the feel of it. Rock back and
forth, letting your shoulders and hips make contact and then
lose contact with the ground. Open your eyes and look at the
sky, the trees, the blossoms if they're out. Feel the moist, cool

soil under you, supporting you and giving you space to flow. Think about being a ball, rolling forward, moving faster, then finally, driving at a dizzying pace toward its goal.

It's time to go. Link your hands, and hold your legs tight together. Shut your eyes again, and let your body begin its descent. Don't let your bones get in your way; think of yourself as a muscle tube, all compact and smooth on the outside. There you go! Rolling, rocking, spinning down the hill, whizzing faster and faster. That *oh-gosh!* feeling in the pit of your stomach is supposed to be there. Clear your mind of everything except the exuberance and delight of the movement that your body is doing all by itself. Let yourself go—don't try to stop!

After a while, you'll sense that the slope of the hill is flattening out, and you are coming to the completion of your ride. Open your eyes. See where you are. (It's typical to go way off course, but if you've plotted your hill in advance, that shouldn't make any difference.) This is a marvelous vacation for a spring day when work is piled up on your desk.

Hills teach us about not trying too hard. Without doing a thing, you are transported into another world where there is no voice mail to return and no obligation to anyone other than yourself.

39 ✲ Sunrise Euphoria

If you're on a vacation, you automatically think about sleeping in. Long, lazy mornings stretched out on the mattress, shades blocking the light, staying in bed until noon just because you can. But a very special vacation can be had by getting up early enough to see a sunrise. It's one of the best ways to appreciate the scope of the day ahead.

You can do this two ways. One is to stay up all night so that you barely notice that you haven't had enough sleep. It's like purposely inducing jet lag. You may crash late in the afternoon and find you have to take a nap, which may mess up your sleep schedule for a couple of days to come. The other, preferred way is to go to bed a little early (not too early, or you won't fall asleep) and set your alarm for 4:30 or 5:00 on a summer night, later at other times of the year. Aim for about fifteen minutes before sunrise.

It will be pitch black when you get up, but you may be able to hear the coo of mourning doves, the earliest birds around. Get dressed and go outside immediately, don't stop for coffee. Don't spend time trying to figure out directions when you're so sleepy that you can barely stand up. Make sure you know where east is before you take this trip: you're going to feel pretty disappointed if you miss the sunrise because you were turned around the wrong way.

Now look at the landscape. If you're standing in front of your home, everything will seem pretty familiar to you—a porch swing, the columns of your house or apartment building, trees or bushes—but the objects will be dim, covered with a barely perceivable veil of shadow. As you stand still, the veil will begin to lift. You will discern details such as the chipped paint, the color of flowers, the peep of a bird. The dark sky will change so slowly that you may think you've imagined it. You'll start to notice signs of life: robins busy with worms, a spiderweb connecting the branch of a tree to the house.

The lightning now comes faster. As you stand still, the sky will seem to grow larger as it shakes off the cloak of night. The houses in your neighborhood are clearly outlined, and the newspaper-delivery car will stagger along the street, raggedly leaning left and right as one arm throws at each house in turn.

It's time. You can feel the heat of the day becoming palpable, sapping the moisture out of the ground. Highlights of crimson flood the sky, as though someone had thrown a paint bucket right across the horizon. Things are moving quickly, and the hot ball of yellow sun jumps up, first just the tip of it, then, majestically, the entire orb. Look away and watch the red drain from the sky as sunlight floods everything and golden streaks appear on driveways and light up puddles.

It's now at least five degrees warmer than when you woke up, maybe ten. The world is beginning to move, the joggers trudging along the streets, the delivery trucks starting on their appointed rounds. Time for you to get going, too—with a whole day ahead of you to remember the terrific show performed just for you at 5:30 this morning.

40 ⚘ The Long Drive Home

Many of us take the same route home day after day. Maybe you leave the office, drive out of the lot, turn right, and start for the highway. Or else you walk to your regular bus or subway stop, or race for the train station along the same street. You see the same things every day, and you become one of the million commuters in the great sea of humanity on the move. It's as regular as clockwork. You don't have to think: you could make this trip blindfolded. You get into that hazy netherworld of moving along, the radio or your Walkman churning out the Top 40, which you know already, your feet or your car covering all that ground you know already, your brain retracing all those circuits it knows already.

Take a vacation today, and go home the long way. On a lovely fall evening, with the leaves a riot of color around you, you have a great opportunity to enjoy the views you never see. Almost as though you got on a plane, landed in another state, and have a chance to explore.

If you have a good sense of direction, you probably have a notion of which way to go. (If you have no one at home waiting to join you for dinner, it doesn't much matter whether you get lost, unless this makes you feel panicky.) Turn off your radio, Walkman, and cell phone, and concentrate only on where you are and where you're going, even if you have no idea where that is.

The only rule of this trip is to go down streets and through areas that you don't really know. If you've lived and worked in one neighborhood for a long time, this is your chance to break out and see another part of your community. It doesn't matter if it's leading you home. Why not get off at a different stop and go see the park with the modern sculpture in it, or the waterfront, or the bird sanctuary? It's cheating yourself never to take advantage of the subtle cultural and ethnic shifts of areas as you move along just a few blocks north and south, east and west.

Taking the long way home also gives you time to process one part of your day before the next part begins. It's a bridge between one of your worlds and the next. You can mellow out, reflect on problems that came up during the day, play around with possible solutions. You can think about what you'd like to do when you get home, who you'd like to spend time with, or if you'd like to be alone.

One of the nice things about a vacation is that no one knows you. You can start over, have an accent, erase your past, be anyone you've ever wanted to be. So, as you journey home, stop at a drugstore or convenience store and buy a pack of gum or a newspaper. Pretend you're from another part of the country, or even a foreign land, and have just discovered this place. See how it feels to look with different eyes at the rather familiar territory you inhabit. Others will see you as a tourist, just wandering through. You will have the pleasure of knowing that you are gathering information for tomorrow, when you just may take another long, circuitous route that will become an adventure before you turn around and head for home.

41 ✶ Starry, Starry Night

It was cloudy in the morning, but the sun burned off the haze, and the late afternoon sky was a perfect, unsullied blue. Even as you hurried around finishing your various tasks for the day, you knew it was going to be a wonderful night, perfect for a vacation.

You can sit on your porch or on the stoop outside your apartment house or up on the roof, unless there's a street lamp right beside you. The farther away you can get from artificial lights, the better. Ideally, you want a black sky as a backdrop for the palette of twinkling, sparkling droplets that form themselves into constellations. If you live in the heart of a city, you can walk over to the local high school and sit in the bleachers beside the playing field.

Let's say you pick a perfect fall evening. You eat a light dinner and then get into your car or start walking as the light begins to fade from the sky. Don't dawdle. The time between sunset and starlight is short, and you can be deceived in the autumn when it's still warm and you recall those summer nights when it didn't get dark until 9:30. Be alert: watch for a few nights from your window, and then give yourself time to get to your perch behind the school.

Look up. You won't see anything happening at first, and then, you'll think your eyes are playing tricks on you. Was that a plane? Is that some kind of satellite orbiting the earth? The basic question to ask when you start seeing lights is: Are they moving? If they are, it's likely *we* put them up there.

Watch for stillness—lights that hover as though a giant hand had just planted them. Is that Orion's belt? You can just make out the two dippers, one linked to the other. If you know the plan of the sky, you can impress yourself with all the constellations you can name. But if you have a beginner's mind and have no idea where anything is, you're ahead of the game. You can pick out your own designs and weave stories from them. Be aware of shapes and patterns: some lights are closer to Earth and therefore brighter; some are so far away that they seem just a reflection of their larger, bolder cousins.

What perspective you can gain when you watch the sky at night! You hold up your hand and look at the scale of that tiny star against it. Except it's the other way around! In reality, your hand is infinitesimally small in comparison with the star. Think about what seeing those lights implies: the fact that we are so small, so insignificant in the great plan of the universe, and yet, we have a full life, replete with ideas, emotions, people, and tasks that we perform—some well, some badly.

There is a softness to the sky's lights that can never be rivaled by a set designer attempting to mimic the display. Feel how the protective covering of night gives you a respite from the day's hassles. When you return from this vacation, it will be with a bigger sense of who you are and why you're here.

42 ❧ Lessons in Earthly Delights

You put a sprout in soil, and you water and fertilize it. It grows. And that gives you the impetus to feed it, nurture it, talk to it. Planting something in a piece of ground or a pot is one of the most positive vacations you can take.

What you plant in your garden, or on your deck or windowsill is irrelevant. Even if you have nothing growing, you can still create a masterpiece. (Think of the restful Zen meditation gardens made of nothing but waving patterns of sand under artfully placed rocks. These can be done outside or in a frame, indoors.) This voyage will fill you with a sense of accomplishment and of great aesthetic pleasure as well. You may have sun or shade, weeds or sand, warm weather or chilly—it doesn't matter. Being close to the earth is valuable, for you and for your plant.

You can get your plant at a nursery, through a mail-order catalog, or in the supermarket. Read the label to find out how to care for the beast: how much water it likes, whether it can get its feet wet (that means, whether you water in the saucer or from above), and whether it likes sun, shade, or a mixture. You'll need a pot slightly larger than the one it came in, some good potting soil, and an all-purpose fertilizer. If you're in an apartment, you need to figure out which window your plant will live in. Remember, you want to have it in view as much as you can during your day. Watching a plant, seeing how it turns to the light, how it puts out new leaves and flowers, how it survives, even when you don't lavish attention on it, is a relaxing and inspiring experience.

Start your twenty-minute vacation by spreading out some newspaper and upending the plant from its temporary pot. Let it lie there with its roots extending around it like a halo as you prepare its new home. If you're working the ground, dig down under, letting the soil aerate and the worms stretch their segmented bodies. If you're planting in a pot, fill it partway with soil, and leave a space in the middle for the roots to stretch down. Place the plant in the hole you've dug or in the center of the pot, and add more soil until it covers all the roots and comes up to the level of the first leaves. Pat the soil firmly around the plant. Then water until you make mud. You may need to pack some more soil around the plant if too much has washed away. If you're working in a pot, let the excess water drain out.

Spend time feeling the cool soil between your fingers, the turgid stems of the plant, and the feathery leaves and flowers that sprout from it. It grows slowly, imperceptibly, relying only on the basics you've provided. Just some soil, sun, water, and a few kind words, and the plant stays healthy and will, in time, divide and make another plant. Your life can be the same as this plant: you need very little in the way of comfort, nourishment, and air to move ahead in the things you want for yourself.

After you've finished your planting, always sit back and breathe in the heady aroma of moist soil and the life that springs out of the earth. Keep your perspective. It's not just a bunch of flowers and leaves: your plant has a personality. It can be your companion in serenity and calm, a spot where you can retreat any time you like.

5
Romantic Respites

Maybe there's no time or money for a delectable rendezvous in St. Bart's or a cruise around the world, but there are lots of little things you two can do to keep the love alive every day.

43 ❧ Hearts United, Limbs Entwined

We've all heard that yoga is good for us, but it's even better—and a lot more touchy-feely—when you can share postures with your sweetie. When the two of you are running around all day, busy working and doing errands, stop for just twenty minutes and share a stretch or two.

Yoga, from the Sanskrit word meaning "yoke" or "union," attempts to unite body, mind, and spirit by twisting the body into various shapes that can be done by one or modified for two. The purpose of yoga is to lay the groundwork for meditation. By assuming standing, sitting, kneeling, and reversed (upside down) postures, you break the conventional mental patterns of what the body is supposed to do and how it's supposed to feel. So, take off your shoes and loosen your belt.

Stretching Out

Start by warming up with a general two-person stretch. Sit on the floor facing each other with legs wide apart, holding hands and touching feet. (If one of you has much longer legs than the other, the shorter person's feet should be on their partner's calves.) Partner A will start to roll down his or her spine, as though about to lie down. Partner B will follow, leaning forward and directing the amount of stretch. If one of you is more flexible than the other, you'll have to accommodate—just like in your relationship. Then switch, and let the other partner roll down onto his or her back. Breathe as you seesaw back and forth. You'll find that you are soon able to open wider and roll down farther than when you started the exercise.

The Warrior

Stand facing each other, just far enough away so that you could lean forward and kiss if you wanted to. (But don't do that yet.) Spread your legs wide apart, and extend your arms way out to each side. Now join hands. Partner A will turn the right foot out and bend the right knee; Partner B will turn the left foot out and bend the left knee as you both stretch to the side on which your knee is bent. Breathe into the posture and hold it. Then come up out of the bent-knee pose, turn the foot parallel again, and repeat to the opposite side.

The Cat and the Fish

Here are two complimentary postures that will get you very close together. Partner A will do the cat, Partner B will do the fish, and then you'll switch.

The Cat On hands and knees, round your back, dropping your head, and roll your spine upward, then arch your neck and back, and return to the starting posture (you will have made a circle with your torso).

The Fish Lie on your back with your arms at your sides. Arch your neck, and lift your upper back off the floor, supporting your weight on your shoulders and the crown of your head.

The Combined Pose Partner B will lie on the floor. Partner A will kneel, straddling B's waist, with hands on the sides of B's upper arms. As B assumes the fish posture, A will begin the cat rolls, and your chests will touch (you can kiss if you like) at the downswing of the cat, since both will be arched.

After you've done this five times, A will become the fish, and B the cat.

The coordination required to put these two postures together is similar to the type of give-and-take that two people need in a romantic partnership. And look at the exercise and flexibility you'll get from just twenty minutes of entwining your bodies as well as your hearts.

44 ✷ Twenty-Minute Tunes

There is nothing more romantic than a love song, especially when you're dancing to it. The music reaches out to you and begs you to cleave to your sweetheart, combine your limbs in some fashion, and sway until the last note dies away. This is what you'll get on your tuneful vacation. Slow dancing for twenty minutes can be blissful.

Love songs have been around since the medieval troubadours composed them for the gallant knights who fought well but didn't have the wit and romantic inclination to impress their lady loves. More modern versions range from Cole Porter and

Irving Berlin to Stephen Sondheim and Leonard Bernstein to Madonna and Garth Brooks. The great thing about this trip is that you don't have any work to do. All the mushy sentiment you need to inspire you to dance is right there in the song.

Spend a few minutes deciding what you want to listen to. (If you pick the right time of night, many of the jazz stations run blocks of slow, deliciously sexy music.) You should take this vacation in a cozy spot: maybe in your bedroom, maybe in your backyard or the rooftop of your building with a boom box playing under a starry sky. Let the first notes draw you closer, then join hands. You can assume a traditional dance position, or you can keep your arms around each other while you sway, eyes closed, relaxing completely into one another's arms.

It's very sexy to slow-dance. Your legs are touching, your hearts beat as one, and there is virtually no space that you don't fill together. The promise of that physical contact is exciting, although it doesn't have to lead anywhere. You can kiss while dancing, or gaze into one another's eyes. While you're holding your partner close, it can be nice to hum to your lover (if you can stay on key!). That makes the connection between you even stronger. On the other hand, you might want to wait until the end of the song, then embrace your sweetie passionately. You may never get to the next number.

Always remember that you are doing this not to perform, but in order to tell your sweetheart just what you think of him or her. We often let months go by before we say, "I love you," or "You're very special to me." This vacation is one way to rectify that error. So, when you move to the music, do it with style and passion. Be aware of the fluctuations of mood and rhythm. Let your body say everything the words of the song are saying.

End your vacation by dancing to a song that has meaning for you both. Maybe there's a love song that was on the radio the night of your first date, or one that's become your theme song over the months or years you've been together. You can feel joyous. It's wonderful to realize that your lives have become as harmonious as the music to which you're dancing. Open your arms, open your hearts, and hold on to each other for dear life.

45 ❧ I Want to Hold Your Hand

It sounds too simple to be erotic, doesn't it? That's because you haven't held hands in a while. Just holding on like that for twenty minutes—nothing else—can be bliss. No buildup to a kiss; no furtive groping at clothes; no rambling, passion-crazed monologue to express your inmost feelings.

Remember the first time you ever touched? Maybe it was an accident—a simple brush of two bodies colliding in space—but when it happened, you were transformed.

The same thing is going to happen right now. You won't want to set the timer for this voyage, but you'll probably be able to guess just how long you've been welded together.

Start by standing or sitting near enough to touch comfortably. Rub your own hands together to get the circulation going. Then hold your hands out to your partner, and make contact. At first, you'll feel silly, and your fingers may grasp too hard. Maybe your hands are cold, maybe they're a little grimy from whatever work you've been doing. Look down and see how your palms join your lover's, how the fingers interlace. One person's hands may be large and rough, and the other's small and fragile, or they may be similar in size and structure. How old are the hands? Are they young and smooth, or can you see the lovely latticework of veins? Are the nails painted? Are the fingers bare, or do they wear rings?

Now examine the way the four hands fit together. A hand lying on a counter or holding a telephone has a certain integrity all its own, but when that hand joins forces with another, it becomes a totally different organ. And when you have two sets of them, they are powerful indeed. Twenty fingers, twenty nails, four palms, and four heels. Many music buffs consider pieces for piano four-hands to be some of the most interesting work for keyboard ever written.

Now close your eyes and see how you feel, being held by those important digits that do so much—the hands that work, prepare meals, wipe up spills, arrange flowers, softly stroke a cheek or a brow, comfort a weeping child, and drive you wild in bed. What is it about these hands that conveys the entire personality of the one you love?

Play together just with your fingers. Let them run in and out between the webbing of your partner's hands. Clap by making the heel of each hand pull away and then jump back together again. Give a massage: use your thumb and fingers to work deeply into the muscles and bones of your partner's hand.

There is an electricity in the air that now seems to be absorbed by your skin. If your hands were clammy and cold at the beginning of this vacation, they are now probably toasty and comfortable, the blood coursing through them. Your hands hover in the air like hummingbirds. Then, as the trip comes to an end, they part oh so delicately. But the feeling and intensity remain long after the touch is gone.

46 ✻ Thanksgiving—Relationship Style

How often do we stop and feel grateful for finding that adorable person whom we spend so much of our time with? After all, it's at least partly chance that we ended up with our current partner. We could have been in another place, at another time, and never met. But thanks to fate, karma, good planning, or an excellent matchmaker, we've got the prize. And this vacation will allow us to take the valuable time to give thanks for what we have.

The real meaning of Thanksgiving is often lost in the commercial hubbub that surrounds it. We've been given one day a year to be reminded of all those things that make us happier, saner, better—and we rarely acknowledge them, even on the holiday. But with a relationship-style Thanksgiving, you can do it any day or night, in any season.

Sit back and think about what it is that attracted you to your object of desire in the first place: a great smile, a sense of humor, an ability to listen well, a pair of luscious lips or great abs? Write it all down. And then, what was it that first made you realize that this person is a keeper—not just a casual acquaintance or date, but someone you had to see and be with all the time?

Try to enumerate the particular ways in which you interact well together. Are you good friends? Good coworkers? Can you decide easily what movie or restaurant you want to go to? (That's important when you care about vacations!) Are you great lovers? House renovators? Talkers? Coparents? It's amazing, when you begin to compile a list, how many things a couple does together.

As your vacation continues, jot down memorable moments you've spent together. Hilarious times, hard times when you felt you had nothing in common except the fact that you needed each other, warm and wonderful times that showed you both how important you were to each other. Are you alike or very different? What do you enjoy about your various similarities and differences?

Then think about what you might do in order to show your partner how much you care. It's no good just assembling all this information if you don't share it. What a great surprise—better than a Christmas present. This type of Thanksgiving will be a gift for the one you love. This is a vacation that does a great deal of good for you and your sweetheart. What a delightful way to spread a little holiday cheer, all year long.

47 ❧ Roll with It

It's one of those mundane Saturdays. You have nothing to do and nowhere to go. The two of you have decided to clean the house until it sparkles, something you haven't done in months. It's dull, exhausting, and incredibly tedious. Your mind eventually turns to thoughts of fun.

As long as you're in the throes of laundry, try this spontaneous and delightful outing for lovers. (You can do it alone, but it's not as much fun.) Strip the bed, and put the sheets and comforter in the dryer on high. About twenty minutes of preparation time—while you continue to do chores—is all you need to get them steamy. You can look forward to the vacation you're about to take with suggestive remarks and a little slap-and-tickle touching while you put away dishes, vacuum, or sort the underwear.

As soon as the timer goes off, race upstairs with the bedclothes, lock the bedroom door just in case the kids come back, and tear off each other's clothes. (You can tear off your own, but it's not as much fun.) Pile the sheets and comforter on the bed, and dive in. Enjoy the delirious sensation of warmth penetrating your arms, legs, face, back, and every body part in between. Roll up your lover, and jump on top, then put the other sheet over you—make a sandwich. Unroll just one limb, and kiss it; lick it; rub it against one of yours. Any and every type of play is encouraged—but remember that you have only twenty minutes. At the end of that time, the sheets will be room temperature again, and your chores may or may not seem to be calling you. Make that bed, and get back to work!

Or, if you like, take them back down to the dryer and start all over again.

48 ✷ Auto Erotic

Car romance is a tried-and-true activity that has sustained many lovers through long periods when they didn't have a place to go. Even if you have a lovely home with four bedrooms in which you could romp, it's sometimes more fun to pretend that you have to scrounge for privacy. If you haven't made out in the backseat since you were sixteen, it's time you caught up with your past. It will bring back fond memories—and will allow you to expand the scope and location of romance in your life.

First, you need to find a spot where you won't be disturbed. The lovers' lanes of old are sometimes too jammed with traffic to be cozy, and some are too remote to be safe, especially at night. (Then too, you don't want trouble with the authorities who may be patrolling the area.) You might consider a new housing development where no one has yet moved in. The simplest idea is to hide in plain sight and tuck yourselves away on a residential block in a line of parked cars. One of the thrills of this kind of cuddling is that you have to make do with what you've got, whatever that is. If you can't take your clothes off, so be it. You can find other ways to distract one another.

First, get in the backseat (depending on the weather, you may need to leave the heater or air conditioner going). It's always a challenge to find a comfortable position. The nice thing about having to make adjustments for the size and shape of the space you're in is that you get to laugh while discovering each other's body in a new way, whether you're sitting, kneeling, or half-lying. One of you can arrange the other so that it feels comfortable for you; then you can switch. And hopefully, you'll find a few positions that you both like. Anyway, it's fun exploring them.

After you're shoehorned in together, don't say a word. This type of experience should feel primal—something that triggers those lusty desires. You can start to touch and kiss, and see where it goes. As you caress each other, knowing that you have a time limitation, you may discover that your desires become more urgent and more passionate. But if it's broad daylight or you're in the middle of a neighborhood, you may feel too self-conscious to consummate the act. That's perfectly all right: you can fondle, grasp, massage, rub, lick, suck, and tickle each other unmercifully for this brief period of time. And that may get your juices flowing for later, when perhaps you'll have the leisure (and location) to pursue all the delights of body, mind, and spirit.

Car romance is, by its very nature, hasty, messy, and delirious. Sometimes the headiest romance comes to a boil in the shortest time.

49 ❋ Voices of Love

When Alexander Graham Bell invented the telephone, he couldn't foresee that almost every household in America would have more than one and many people would carry them at all times. But they're very useful for a quick trip to lovers' lane—and you don't even have to leave the house! In this vacation, you're going to call your darling and tell him or her all your hopes, dreams, and wishes for an ideal date. When you hang up twenty minutes later, you'll be filled with the derring-do to act out a semblance of what you had in mind.

It's difficult for many people to express themselves romantically when they're face to face with someone they care about. Most of us feel that it's embarrassing or awkward to talk about intimate matters and say what we really mean. Somehow, we all have a notion of being judged when someone looks at us. Suppose the other person laughs? Suppose he or she doesn't feel quite the same way you do? Because of these reservations, it's often easier to whisper sweet nothings in your partner's ear when he or she isn't present. The telephone, especially late at night in a darkened room, has the aura of a church confessional: no one can see you, and you're safe to say anything, feel anything.

Call your sweetie and offer some hot suggestions for what you might do when you're together. If you happen to be home together, pick up one of your extensions and titillate your partner. (It's even more exciting knowing how close he or she is.) Talking in a romantic way is sometimes even better than doing anything overtly sexual. You can use "dirty" words or a language made up of terms that have special meaning to the two of you. You can concoct an ideal date that you couldn't possibly afford: a carriage ride around Central Park followed by a candlelit dinner in your room at the Plaza Hotel, capped off with a memorable night making love on a bed of five dozen thornless red roses. You can take your love on a plane anywhere in the world, or simply imagine what it would be like to have a whole weekend free of chores.

Flirting on the phone is a great way to recharge your romantic batteries because this activity exploits the really sexy organ: the brain. Your mind has no limitations, so anything at all is possible.

When your darling picks up, start with an introduction. Pretend that you've never met before, or that you've only seen each other in passing. Listen to the sound of the other's voice as though you were hearing it for the first time. Is it high or low? Raspy or smooth? What's the timbre of the voice like? You might want to describe yourself physically (emphasizing your best features), or tell your lover that you happened to spot him or her on the street the other day and were struck dumb with attraction. Be sure to say *why* you find your lover so appealing—it's nice to feel wanted and flattered. Ask whether he or she is free on Friday at 7:00, or in an hour.

You can then go on to describe exactly what you have in mind, but leave a few spaces blank so that your sweetie can fill them in. Maybe you know that you'd like to take your lover away for a weekend, but you're not sure where he or she dreams of going. You can talk about certain clothing (or lack of clothing) that drives you wild. Maybe you can conjure a scenario for the two of you to act out when you meet.

Finally, you can laugh together. Humor is one of the things that make us feel warm toward the person we love. This collaboration of minds and hearts is one twenty-minute trip you won't want to miss.

50 ✷ Strip Monopoly

Monopoly, of course, is a game of wheeling, dealing, and power brokerage. You can get rich quick or lose everything (or both) in the scope of an hour or two. When you think about it, romance is similar to the ups and downs of the real estate market: if you don't take a chance on love, nothing happens; if you do take a chance, well, you can lose your heart or gain the world.

You've probably been playing Monopoly since you were a kid, but this interpretation adds a little zing. You're still going to move around the board, buying and selling houses and utilities, but every time you pass "Go," or when you get one of those clunker cards, such as "Go to Jail" or "Luxury Tax," you have to let your partner remove one piece of your clothing, likewise if you get a card that requires you to pay any fines or interest. You can remove one sock and one shoe at a time, but jewelry doesn't count. Since you're going to be playing for only twenty minutes (the person with more clothes on at the end wins), you don't have to worry too much about looking indecent when you put your first house on the property you own. But that outcome is possible, particularly in the hot weather, when you aren't wearing much to start with.

Start the game, as usual, by dealing $1,500 to each player: two each of $500s, $100s, and $50s; six $20s and five $10s, $5s, and $1s. The rest of the money goes to the bank.

Each player rolls the dice, and the one with the higher number starts. Let's imagine you start, with your token on the spot marked "Go." Naturally, your partner will take one piece of clothing off of you to start the game off right. Then you'll roll the dice and make your move. If you land on a property, you can purchase it, and once you've nabbed all the lots of one color, you can buy houses or hotels, just as in the regular game. But if you draw a Chance or Community Chest card, you may have to remove some clothing. If you go to jail, pay a doctor's fee (this is appropriate, since you undress for the exam), or even win a prize in a beauty contest (since you wouldn't be wearing a lot of clothes when you won, after all), another piece comes off. On the other hand, you can win back pieces of clothing if you get bonuses—if your Christmas fund matures, or if you receive an income tax refund.

Players can make deals, just as they do in life. Private transactions may be negotiated on unimproved properties, railroads, and utilities, for any amount the owner can get. And, should you decide you wish to peel off more clothing from your partner than is coming off in the course of the game, you can plunk down a few extra dollars for that, too.

If you should happen to land on Boardwalk or Park Place, you can buy back your clothing for $100 per piece. But why be a spoilsport? It's more fun to relax with your sweetheart in the almost-altogether.

51 ✻ Cyber-Love

Letters used to be the glue that cemented two people who were falling in love. Think Abelard and Heloise; think Elizabeth Barrett Browning and Robert Browning, or George Sand and Chopin. History is made of these epistolary romances—and we can recreate them today, in much less time and with much less effort, simply by sending passionate E-mail.

The Internet has opened a vast new world of communication. And there's nothing as sexy as finding that wonderful message—"You've Got Mail"—and discovering it's from the one you love.

Twenty minutes a day should give you ample time to read the love letter that's been sent to you and respond. You could share a fantasy, or tell each other a few X-rated wishes. Since this can sometimes be embarrassing, you can always couch your comments by describing them as dreams. The content of many dreams is extremely sexual: we allow ourselves images and acts that we would never permit ourselves while awake. If you get into these with your partner, you may be surprised as to how close the two of you can get to making fantasy into reality.

You don't have to be a master of the English language or any other to make this an exciting vacation. If the two of you don't fancy yourselves as writers, you may want to communicate in code. This is also advisable if you're sending mail from a large corporate electronic system, since we all know that the Internet is not particularly secure, and you don't want anyone else reading your love letters. The two of you can make up some phrases that send a specific message of what you have in mind for later on. So, "The dog is on fire" could mean "I want to make love to you," and "The lawn mower is always green" could mean "I miss you so much."

You might also express your gratitude for having such a wonderful person in your life. Instead of filling your message with ideas about what to do or where to go, step back and tell your partner what it is about him or her that makes you delirious, or calms you down, or makes you laugh out loud (LOL in cyber-terms).

Don't send your E-mail at the same time every day. Let it be a total surprise, whether it's a long epistle or just those three little words. The point of sending these messages is to show your partner that you're thinking of the two of you together even when you're far apart.

52 ❧ Herbal Erotica

To enhance the feeling between you in just twenty minutes is a challenge, but herbs can turn the tide and safely, soundly, make you feel a little more desirous and passionate. Herbs are probably the oldest pharmaceutical medicines that exist. You can utilize the whole plant—the seeds, flowers, bark, rhizome, and root—and each part of it will give you some benefit.

But remember that herbs don't work like pills. In general, it takes about three months to make a considerable change in your system if you're ingesting herbs in the form of tea, infusion, or tincture. You can, however, derive twenty wonderful minutes of romantic delight from concocting and then drinking a potion using an herbal base that will definitely put you "in the mood."

Herbs and spices have been used in cooking and in the bedroom from time immemorial. The various chemicals from the plant we're using may relax or stimulate us and heighten our anticipation of what's to come. This herbal benefit goes right to the limbic system of the brain, that primitive area that is responsible for memory, emotion, and sexual appetite. They are particularly effective when consumed about an hour before lovemaking.

Here are a few love potions to drive you and your partner wild. Amanda McQuade Crawford, director of the California School of Herbal Studies, developed these delicious cocktails.

Vanilla Rose Cordial

The rose is a symbol of love; vanilla is a stimulating and aphrodisiac spice.

> 1 pound fresh or 4 ounces dry rose petals
> 2 ounces vanilla extract, or 4 vanilla beans
> 4 ounces Vitex (Chaste-berry)
> 4 ounces damiana
> 1 liter brandy
> Honey (to taste)

Thoroughly mix all ingredients in a large container with a tight-fitting lid. Store the mixture in a cool, dry place for two weeks, shaking daily. Strain and bottle the cordial. When you're ready to consume your potion, stir one to three tablespoons of the cordial into a glass of cold sparkling mineral water.

Red-to-Orange Chakra Express

> 1 ounce ground allspice
> ¼ ounce whole cloves
> 1 ounce cinnamon sticks
> 2 ounces astragalus

1 ounce ground nutmeg

2 ounces ginger root

1 ounce fennel seeds

1 ounce star anise

1 ounce bay leaves

¼ ounce guarana (optional—Brazilian aphrodisiac, high in
  caffeine)

2 bottles Beaujolais or burgundy wine

Place all ingredients in a container with a tight-fitting lid.
Refrigerate for two weeks. Leave all leaves, sticks, and bark in
the wine for maximum potency. When you're ready to imbibe,
strain off a wineglass full, and allow it to come to room
temperature. Enjoy!

6
Cultivate the Mind

*I*f you want a vacation that challenges you and gets you thinking, you might undertake a museum tour of Europe, or an anthropological dig in Africa. On the domestic scene you might sign up for an adult-education course at a local community college. These, however, are major commitments. But with ingenuity, you can improve your IQ and learn some new skills when you have only a little time available, absorbing information and knowledge each day.

53 ❧ A Puzzling Getaway

You don't even need the newspaper to tease your brain. You can create your own crossword puzzle and delve to the depths of your linguistic ability. How about a word square that reads the same down as across? Start with a grid of four, and you'll get something like this:

P	L	A	Y
L	O	R	E
A	R	E	A
Y	E	A	R

To create your brainteaser, choose a simple word as your anchor, and lay it out both vertically and horizontally. Go down to the next letter, and work a word around it. Let's start with the word *plan* instead of *play*. Instead of *lore*, you might have chosen *lane*. For the third word, we'll substitute a proper name, *Anne*, which works nicely. Instead of *year*, try *need*. You can fiddle around with words that will match and see what you come up with. Here's our revised grid:

P	L	A	N
L	A	N	E
A	N	N	E
N	E	E	D

If this type of patterning is too tight-laced for you, you can free up your crossword vacation. Draw a set of horizontal and vertical boxes, one for each letter. Start with a grid that measures five by five. (If this is too easy for you, you can try six by six or seven by seven.)

Write the letters of the alphabet on individual slips of paper, then scramble them. Reach into the pile, pick out your first letter, and place it anywhere on your grid. Pick another letter, and put it into the grid. At the end of the round (twenty-five letters have been chosen), you will have some lines, both vertical and horizontal, with complete words, and some that have complete words and extra letters added on. After all your boxes are completely filled, add up your score. You get a point for each letter in a real word, spelled out either horizontally or vertically. For example, D-R-E-A-M would give you 5 points, and E-A-R-N-P would give you 4. If you happened to get A-N-D-E-S, you'd get 5 points, but you wouldn't get an additional 3 points for A-N-D, contained within your major word.

You'll now have something that looks like this:

W   O   M   A   N   ("woman" gives you 5 points—you can't use "man" or "oman" too!)

H   A   D   Z   S   ("had" or "adz" gives you 3 points)

I   B   M   L   C   (no points)

L   U   L   L   W   ("lull" gives you 4 points)

E   N   B   A   D   ("bad" gives you 3 points)

Scoring down, "while" gives you 5 points, and "bun" gives you 3 points, but you get no points for the other vertical rows reading down. Scoring up, "Eli" gives you 3 points, "nub" gives you 3, and "all" gives you 3. You get no points for the other two vertical rows reading up.

You can continue to challenge yourself by adding squares to your grid, and you can also spend twenty minutes on today's newspaper crossword. Just keep in mind, whichever form of word game you're playing, that it's a good idea to avoid words that give you P-A-I-N or S-T-R-E-S-S.

54 ✤ Kidding Around

Reading to a child could be the single most beneficial vacation you ever take—bar none. It's good for you, good for the child, and good for the future of our civilization. The more we read, the more knowledge we can absorb, and the more we are stimulated to think seriously about signifcant issues.

And this starts young. (There are those conscientious parents who read to their kids while they're still in the womb—and others who start the process on the first day of life.) Even if you wait a year or so, reading to a child makes good sense. If you can catch a kid's imagination early, you'll have a curious youngster who will say, "Please, tell me the story again! Show me the pictures! Why did that happen to the main character? Do you think it was fair?" Or maybe just one who says, "I love reading."

Now, there's a trick to this vacation. You can't just do your job of reading words and showing pictures. You have to be the story: you have to spark that fire by creating an atmosphere of wonder and excitement. You can do that with your voice.

If you're going into this pursuit as a first-time reader, you have a beginner's mind. You don't do this on a regular basis, so you haven't made any mistakes yet. If you're going into this as a sometime reader looking for tips, be happy! You can definitely improve in a flash: just one twenty-minute mind trip will take you there.

Begin by selecting a story you love. There are some extraordinary children's books out there that span the age range, from Tomi di Paola to Dr. Seuss, from A. A. Milne to Judy Blume. The books that are closest to your interests as well as to those of the children you're reading to will hold everyone's attention better.

Once you've selected the book, leaf through it. Get an idea of the illustrations (you'll want to stop frequently, if not at every page, to allow the child to see the picture and maybe discuss it with you), the story line, and the characters. It's the dialogue of those characters that you'll want to hone in on.

One reason that people love to read is that they feel they can actually see the story taking place in front of them. At a younger age, we want a full palette of fascinating people to parade before us. How do you, as the reader, manage to create a cast of characters that are believable? The answer is that you bring them to life with the timbre of your voice.

If you're stumped for "voices," start with those you know well. Don't be reticent about mimicking yourself or anyone you know. Remember, imitation is the sincerest form of flattery. Give a young character in the book a childlike voice; a man, a gruff one; a woman, a melodious one. Or go the opposite route, casting against type. If all the characters are animals, as is often the case, you can have a field day: one can sound whiny and nasal (talk through your nose), one can sound thoughtful and wise (slow your words down), and one can sound tough and nasty (pretend you're reading someone the riot act, and make your words definitive).

Take care to set the scene well. Make sure that when you talk about a sunny day with the flowers blooming, your voice is cheerful and upbeat. When a character is getting into trouble, let your voice convey suspense and anxiety. Don't rush your words because you're embarrassed about your acting ability and just want to "get through it." Take your time, and think about what you're saying.

Just as you want to stop to enjoy the illustrations, you also want to take time to let the child jump in and add to the story, object to some element, or laugh about the characters' predicament. If there's a sad or frightening part in the book, stop to find out how the child feels about this particular emotion. If you have a book in which one phrase is repeated a lot, stop at the phrase after a few times to see if your listener can fill in the blanks. And don't be afraid to editorialize: if you want to comment on the action, or ask the child what he or she thinks is happening, go right ahead.

It's tough to get children to sit quietly these days. Their attention spans have been compromised by tv and the Internet. Television programmers run segments of only fifteen minutes before a station break because that's the extent of most people's concentration! And of course, on the Web, you can switch screens instantly with the click of a mouse. With these two types of media, it's all done for you—the pictures, the story, the interactive games are given to the participant. Reading, on the other hand, demands work on the part of the listener as well as the reader, and this is why a storytelling trip is a vital excursion for everyone involved. If we are to have individuals in the next generation who think for themselves and dream great dreams, we need to retain the wonder of the written and spoken word.

So, get your kids' books out, and open some minds. It's a trip that can lead to new worlds.

55 ✹ In Love with Shakespeare

He's probably the most quoted playwright and poet in the English language. Everyone can toss off "To be or not to be," or "My kingdom for a horse," but who can recite every word of an entire soliloquy from one of his plays or an entire sonnet of his poetry? You can! You're going to memorize a whole piece of Shakespeare to wow your friends, impress your family, and convince yourself that you have something on the ball.

If you haven't memorized anything since you were in high school, you'll need a plan to get a particular set of words to stick in your mind. Memorization is not difficult, but you have to attack it systematically. Shakespeare himself has given you a lot of wonderful aids to make your vacation easier—a challenge rather than a chore.

First, head to a library or look around your own bookshelves for a copy of the Bard's work. Let's examine a sonnet. Pick the one that most appeals to you. Look at the shape of the poem. It has fourteen lines, and the pattern of rhyme is *abab, cdcd, efef, gg.* When you're committing the poem to memory, you have to know where—at the end of which line—a word will sound like another word.

Next, what's the poem about? In one way or another, Shakespearean sonnets deal with love, the fleeting beauty of youth, a trusting heart, or grieving for the past (another reminder of *tempus fugit*-ing). Once you have a general picture of the subject matter, it's easier to put the pieces together.

Proceed to the verses themselves. What images or plays of words strike you? One of the simplest sonnets to memorize is probably "Music to hear, why hear'st thou music sadly" (Sonnet 8) because of the many musical words—*concord, well-tuned sounds, ear, string, note,* and *sing*—as well as the repeated comparisons to marriage and family.

"Shall I compare thee to a summer's day" (Sonnet 18), perhaps the best known of Shakespeare's sonnets, is easy to follow because it describes summer in an inspiring and picturesque way. "When to the sessions of sweet silent thought" (Sonnet 30) is easy to remember because of the sibilance of the *s*'s. If you're a visual person, take a few minutes to jot down the important words or phrases. You can glance down at these every once in a while if you get stuck.

All of us have different learning styles. If you think about yours, you'll become aware of ways in which it's easiest for you to absorb new information. Some of us do well reading things

silently over and over; others by repeating things out loud. Then
there are mnemonic devices, those little catchphrases you design
that trigger an image accessible to your memory. Some people
do well writing things down, copying the sonnet over multiple
times.

Right now, let's try the oral route for Shakespeare, whose
poetry flows beautifully off the tongue. Read the first two lines
aloud several times in succession. Speaking aloud helps memorization because you are actually listening to yourself, as
opposed to just imagining the words inside your head. The
sound and pacing of the lines and the clear ring of the rhymes
are apparent only when the words are voiced.

You can also use a tape recorder if you like. Read the sonnet slowly into the machine, leaving large silences in between
each line, then play back a couple of lines at a time. Alternate
saying them and listening to them (you can mouth the words
while you listen to yourself).

Repeat the first two lines until you've got them, then add
two more. Stop every once in a while to think of the meaning
of the words you're saying. By understanding exactly what's
going on, your brain can make sense of the sequence of words.
You don't want them just to sound good; you want them to ring
with logic and clarity.

Keep adding lines and building toward the whole as you
progress. If you miss a word, go back and think of what else is
in that line. What word would make sense to you there? Try to
fit something in before consulting your book.

Finally, make yourself say the whole thing, start to finish,
with gaps where you forget. Keep a lilting rhythm in your
speech: pretend you know it all even if you're unsure. Repeat
one more time. The more you do it, the more confident you'll
feel. The joy of reading aloud is enhanced when you know the
words. And won't your friends be impressed?

56 ❋ Drawing Down the Moon

It's good for the mind to tackle physical challenges, and one of the most interesting is a geometrical brainteaser in which you are given the challenge of drawing the figure in front of you without crossing or retracing a line or lifting your pencil from the paper. Here are three forms to confound you:

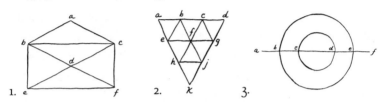

Solutions:

1. Take the following route: E-B-D-C-B-A-C-F-D-E-F.

2. Start with C, and take the following route: C-D-J-F-H-J-K-E-F-B-E-A-C-F.

3. Take the following route: A to B; by upper curve to E; to D; by upper curve to C; straight line to D; by lower curve to C; straight line to B; by lower curve to E; to F.

57 ❋ Mind over Matter

When you were in school, memorizing dates and battles, states and their capitals, or the lineup of presidents was probably a chore. You had to learn all this stuff by rote and then regurgitate it on a test. How dull and difficult. Thankfully, as an adult, you don't have to cram too many extraneous facts into your head.

But you can use the power of your mind to incorporate some interesting facts that will amuse your friends and make you a more desirable dinner guest. That is, if you use a vacation to learn the right stuff. Why not try memorizing the Best Picture, Best Actor/Actress and Supporting Actor/Actress Oscar winners for the last thirty years, or the stats on your favorite baseball player?

Taking this type of vacation is an excellent choice for someone who is into his or her hobby and wants to share it. It's fascinating, for instance, to look back at actors who are now at the top of the Hollywood heap and remember the small roles they once played. You may even reap monetary rewards: for example, knowing everything about a champion ballplayer allows you to make better bets on his team when the World Series comes around. And at the end of this trip, you'll feel smarter and other people will stand amazed at your mental prowess.

How do you memorize your list? First, you have to be dedicated and focused. Sit for a moment and clear your mind. See the inside of your right and left hemispheres as two big rooms. You are now going to take a broom and sweep the debris aside so that you have room to work. As you imagine this sweeping process, clear a space in the middle and see yourself opening your reference book and pouring the contents of your desired list onto the floor in front of you. Ok, you're ready to start learning.

Now you need to find some common theme that will act as an anchor for your memorization process. Many medical students who need to learn hundreds of muscles, bones, and enzymes, etc. for their exams are fans of mnemonic devices, which are a clever way of creating your own personal word or sentence out of the first letters of all the elements you want to remember. With a grouping as large as forty movies, or twice that many movie stars, you'll need several mnemonics. Writing is also a great way to remember something. So copy your list as many times as you can in twenty minutes.

With baseball stats, you have the challenge of numbers. These are best engraved into the brain by rote: just go over them time and again. You can write them out and stick them on your refrigerator so you'll see them every time you walk through the kitchen, or you may want to record them on a tape recorder and play them to yourself while you sleep.

All of these techniques work only if you work them. If you're motivated and focused, you'll find the material sinking in. And so what if you don't get every single actor or number of home runs? It's a vacation—so, take it easy!

58 ✳ Art History 101

You may not know much about art, but you know what you like when you see it. There's something about a painting or sculpture that appeals to your aesthetic sense. It makes you feel good, or makes you laugh, or brings you deep inside yourself and allows you to ponder the larger issues of human life. On this vacation, you may select a period or a painter or sculptor you've always been interested in but never taken the time to appreciate. Your twenty-minute vacation will take you on-line to investigate the amazing galleries of the Louvre in Paris, the Metropolitan Museum in New York, or the Sistine Chapel in Rome.

We often leaf through art books or walk through museums as if we were passengers in a car, watching the scenery pass by without paying much attention to it. What you're going to do on this trip, instead, is concentrate and allow your eye to be your guide to a new world. If you have no idea where to start, you might browse through the galleries at random and pause when you get to something that seems to beckon you, inviting more careful investigation. This is easy to do on a website, since the museums' layouts are offered as soon as you log on, and you are guided through the floors from one room to the next. Or you can go directly to a particular period or work of art and study that one.

Try the Metropolitan Museum of Art in New York City by logging on to www.metmuseum.org/, or travel to Paris and check out the Louvre Museum at www.smartweb.fr/louvre/. You could click on www.vatican.va/ to see the collections of the Vatican Museums in Rome and from there, get to Michelangelo's famous ceiling. Your choices are as diverse as your moods, the artists who are represented, and the attention you devote to them. You might try Islamic art on a day when you crave a sparkling mosaic, some delicate Early American landscapes when you have had too much of the city, a collection of Degas horse sculptures when you want to see movement in clay, or the Mona Lisa—*la Gioconda*—the real thing, as opposed to the zillions of copies you've looked at over the years.

What is it about great art that is worth more than a glance? Perhaps it's the way a particular painter uses light or the quirky way the artist fills every space on the canvas. Maybe it's the story told by the picture or the magnetic look that passes between two of the figures in the canvas. If you like sculpture, you probably stopped because of the amazing similarity of the clay or marble to real life.

Fine art also brings us up short when we think about what we consider "beautiful" or "ugly." Our culture has given us a particular idea of the way the body is supposed to look, for example, but when you go back through the centuries and see what other civilizations found aesthetically pleasing, you may find that you are able to revise your stereotypical attitudes. Look at the lush female bodies of Hindu religious art, or the flat, poignant faces of Flemish madonnas. The squat bodies of Central American sculptures have enormous power, and the strange, distorted shapes of nonrepresentational painting and sculpture take the human face and body to a different dimension.

You might also think about how you see history through the background of paintings. In a fifteenth-century pietà, you will see what the artist's country of origin looked like at that time, and how people dressed, as opposed to the look of the Holy Land where the scene would actually have taken place. In a modern painting—say, a street in a small town in New Jersey by Edward Hopper—you can make comparisons between art and life. How much do they match? How disparate are they? If *you* were to paint that street today, what details would you put in?

On this vacation, you will find your philosophies challenged and your way of viewing the world expanded. If you keep an open mind, your own vision will become clearer and more perceptive.

You may even be inspired to go on a longer vacation later and paint or sculpt your own work of art!

59 ❧ Family Heritage

Every family has its own wonderful, quirky traditions. Of course you've been told how Grandpa Joe walked five miles in the snow to get to school (uphill each way!) and never missed a day. Or the one about how Uncle Ted built a log cabin with his bare hands during the hottest summer on record. These stories have probably become legends in your family.

On this vacation, you're going to create your own legend, one that you'll be able to pass down to your children and your children's children. Remember how much fun it was to hear your grandparents describe life before indoor bathrooms, central heating, electric lights, telephones, and televisions? You can record your own deeds and interesting anecdotes, which may not seem unusual to you but which will make your younger friends and relatives marvel.

Remember when you still had a party line on the telephone? Some families shared the same number, so when you dialed, the operator had to intervene to find out who you were trying to reach. And even when you didn't share a number, you could dial your own number and listen in on conversations over the connection that came through the busy signal.

Remember the day when you got your first TV back in the 1950s, and half the neighborhood came over to watch Milton Berle? There were only a few shows on then: the kids watched Kukla, Fran, and Ollie and Howdy Doody, and the grown-ups had the news with John Cameron Swayze (he advertised Timex watches). After the 11 P.M. news, there just wasn't anymore TV; you got an American flag and finally, a black screen.

And think about the food you ate. There were no McDonald's or Burger Kings. If you wanted a hamburger, you went to a diner. Ice cream didn't come in thirty flavors, just five or six, and you went to the local drugstore to have the soda jerk behind the counter make up your malted, egg cream, or float.

Perhaps you remember pre-computer days when writing college or high school papers involved lots of messy whiteout instead of the handy "delete" key. Vinyl records and eight-track tapes were your music choices and only a few lucky friends had their MTV. Remember making popcorn without a microwave? How about life before answering machines, ATMs, and VCRs? Your descendants and younger friends will be amazed that you survived without the so-called basics.

After you've spent fifteen minutes jotting down the great "firsts" from your past, bring the story up to the present day. You can document your family history with tidbits about upgrading from Atari to Nintendo or the exciting day you traded in your used Volkswagen Beetle for a brand new Toyota Corolla.

Of course, family history is not just made of things. It's a lot more than that. You might end your legacy with an anecdote about the first time you fell in love or the first time you looked at your newborn baby. These pieces of your past can help you build a bridge between the last generation and this one, and offer a wonderful picture of history to your own kids.

60 ❧ Compose Yourself

"Music hath charms to soothe the savage breast." We all know how potent melody and harmony can be, but do we make use of their power in everyday life? On this vacation, you're going to listen—really listen—to one work of one composer whom you particularly admire.

Some people keep the radio on all the time as company. They hardly have any awareness of what the deejay is playing or what the host is talking about. They give in to the common tendency to use music as background noise or company to stave off loneliness. They rarely, if ever, stop to examine what it is about those certain sounds that attracts them.

To make up for this lack, on this vacation, you're going to bring music to the forefront of your consciousness. Start by deciding on a style of music: classical, jazz, folk, rock, or pop. If you're looking for intricacy of composition, think about the first two categories, which tend to be more varied in structure and texture. Bach, Beethoven, Schumann, or Berlioz will give you twenty solid minutes of discovery, as will Mingus, Duke Ellington, or Billie Holiday. (You can have a lot of fun with rock and roll, but it's harder to pick apart the elements because the beat predominates over everything else.)

What surprises us about music is the amazing variation on many levels. There's changing pitch (which makes melody), there's dynamics (how loud or soft it gets), rhythm (on or off the beat), tempo (how fast or slow it is), and harmony (how many complementary notes sound when the major note sounds, and how they change). There's the orchestration or arrangement (the choice of instrument used). A voice and a drum will give a different feeling to the piece in question than a violin and a tuba. Why do you like or dislike the choices the composer has made? If you could rewrite it, would you do it softer, faster, in a higher or lower range?

Now, as you're listening, pay attention to the architecture of the piece. Classical music composition typically uses an *a-b-a* structure. There's a Part One (which may be embellished and decorated), Part Two (which may modulate to another key), and then the repetition and consolidation of Part One. In simple terms, you can think of it as the chorus, the verse, and the chorus again. See if you can guess when the changes come before they actually happen.

What mood does this piece convey? Is it sad, happy, turbulent and heartfelt, or staid and intellectual? Does it tell a story, or is it just a general wash of sound? What is it about the music that gives you this impression? What effects can happen in sound that are as expressive as if you'd conveyed them in words?

As the piece comes to an end, sit for a moment and recapitulate it in your mind. Do you feel different emotionally than you did before you listened to the selection? Music is so evocative of different times and places that we can easily feel as if we've entered into a different world in only twenty minutes. And sometimes it's hard to anchor ourselves to the present and come back again.

If you're a rock fan, you can use these techniques too. The persistent beat in rock, heavy metal, or pop can't be denied. It's not enough to sit and listen to this music; you have to let it take you over. As you feel the rhythm in your body, you can get up and walk to it, sit at the computer and type to it, or even brush your teeth or chop vegetables to it. It can become part of you. What you want to try and do is assimilate the meaning of the music into your own life and see how you, too, can become more harmonious, melodious, and balanced.

When you take your listening skills on a musical vacation, they come back refreshed, ready to pick up on the subtleties of timbre, voice, and inflection of speech. And that can lead to better relationships with everyone you know.

61 ⋇ Take Me Out to the Ball Game

You hated gym in school and never went out for extracurricular team sports. But now you feel left out when everyone crowds around the water cooler and talks about last night's game. Is it too late to learn a little about just one sport? Of course not.

For twenty minutes, take a trip to watch one period of one game that you know nothing about. You have a lot to choose from: it might be football, baseball, basketball, ice hockey, soccer, or even lacrosse or rugby. You can watch the game on TV or head to your local park, playground, or school to get the flavor of it from a local team. If you'd like, you can drag along a friend who knows the score so that you'll have a play-by-play description of what's happening. But if you want to be adventuresome, just take this journey alone and see what happens. You probably won't become an expert, but you'll pay closer attention.

This vacation is about having a beginner's mind. Even if everyone else in America knows the rules of baseball or football, you are starting from scratch. You don't have to come in at the beginning of the game; just dive in anywhere. First, notice how many players there are on a team. Look at the field, court, or rink. How big is it, and what are its characteristics? Are there goals or bases? Is there one player at either end ready to catch a ball or deflect it? How do the teams line up? Do they take solo turns (a pitcher at bat who runs bases, as in baseball), or do they all work together at the same time (basketball players having assigned positions vis-à-vis the other team and where they stand on the court)?

Now begin to look at the ins and outs of the game as far as you can tell. When the ball is in motion, what constitutes a good play? When is a point made? What constitutes a foul? In other words, what stops the action and causes the referee to yell and the players to regroup? Look at the two teams as they scuffle together or prevent one another from being successful. Do they seem to respect the other guys? Or are they out for blood?

Watch the crowd's reaction. Enjoy the energy of the fans, which is sometimes thrilling, sometimes furious. Pick one side to cheer along with even if you aren't quite sure why you're rooting for this team. You'll find that being part of a group of people who are giving their hearts and souls to the team is infectious, and that it's fun to get into the spirit of this excited crowd.

If you're having this vacation in front of the TV, turn off the sound and simply watch. Look at the elegance of a particular player in motion—how fast he throws a ball, how he catches it against all odds (and when everyone else is trying to knock him down). Look at his body in movement, and see the solid physical grace that constitutes a professional athlete. These men and women, thanks to years of training and play, may have numerous injuries and physical problems, but the sound of the words "Play ball!" makes them forget every ache or pain they ever had.

The beauty of their strength, flexibility, and skill is a wonder to see, whether or not you understand anything about what they're up to. For twenty minutes, you can simply enjoy the spectacle.

7

Gourmet Getaways

You could spend a fortune and gain a ton letting a knowledgeable guide take you on an eating tour of Italy or a noshing walk around the Lower East Side of Manhattan. But you can do it yourself, with far fewer calories, very close to home.

62 ❧ Smooth Away the Worries

If we all ate better, we would have more energy to get through the day and wouldn't need breaks as often. Healthy eating, of course, is not everyone's choice of a vacation, although one of the nicest ways to indulge yourself also ends up benefiting your body. Here's a trip to a yummy place where you don't have to worry about the fat content—or the caffeine.

If you imbibe a few diet sodas and a few cups of coffee and gobble an occasional candy bar during the day, you are overwhelming your system with caffeine. Caffeine won't kill you, but most of us ingest far too much of it. It revs us up, stimulating the brain for about an hour, then letting us down fast as blood levels return to normal. Most people make the offense worse by partnering the coffee with a sweet treat such as a cookie, candy bar, or sticky bun, which bump up blood sugar but, once again, offer only a temporary respite from lethargy. It's like being on an energy roller coaster all day long: you never really get a break because you're always reaching for the next "fix."

Let's escape for just twenty minutes via a "smoothie." This delicious, energy-filled treat gives you the benefit of the daily requirement of fruits and vegetables and also offers a vacation from bad coffee breaks. And it takes virtually no time to prepare.

The nice thing about a smoothie is that you can always change what goes into it. Some days, you may crave the rich flavor of a banana; other days, you may want to substitute cranberry or apple for orange juice. You can use fresh fruits when they're in season, such as mangoes, papayas, or blackberries, and simply load up on ice to make the smoothie thick. You can put in sweet vegetables such as carrots, sweet potatoes, and squashes, which increase the health content of your drink. In the winter, you can use frozen fruits and vegetables right from your supermarket freezer section.

By concocting something interesting for yourself, you are not only taking a much needed vacation from your standard menu, but you are also giving your mouth a revitalizing reminder that fresh food really tastes good. When you spend time exploring the various flavors and textures of these smoothies, you actually drink less because each sip means more.

Ingredients:

    1 cup any type fruit, fresh or frozen—choose one or mix
        and match
    ¾ cup of low-fat vanilla yogurt

½ cup orange, apple, cranberry, grape, watermelon, or any
other type of juice (do not use prepared juice mixtures
that contain corn syrup as a sweetener)
5 baby carrots, cut in half lengthwise (you may substitute
squash or sweet potato)
2 heaping tablespoons soy protein (available in health food
stores)
Chipped ice

Combine all ingredients except ice in a blender and blend
until smooth. Add ice chips to thicken. Chill the mixture. Serve
in a beautiful goblet with a sprig of mint or twist of lemon.

Yield: 2 large smoothies, about 150 calories each

63 ❦ A New Taste Sensation

Sometimes we like what we know. That's certainly true in
terms of food. Although manufacturers and marketing special-
ists spend entire careers trying to introduce new products for
people to eat, mostly, our diets don't change much. If you ate
grilled cheese and tomato sandwiches for lunch as a kid, you'll
probably still like that food when you're grown.

On this vacation, you're going to go a little wild and try
some new items that are not part of your regular diet. When
you travel outside your regular orbit, you know that you may
not be able to get the comfort food of home. And it's wonderful to try new things. It gives range to your menu preparation,
and in addition, allows you to get vitamins and minerals from
many different sources. People who eat a varied and diversified
diet tend to maintain a healthy weight, because they are experimenting rather than gorging themselves when they sit down at
the table.

You can spend part of your twenty-minute vacation consulting cookbooks of other lands to get a notion of what you

might like to try. Then add those items to your shopping list, and go get them. Make it a point to purchase one a week. We often avoid the experience of a new food because we imagine what it's going to taste like without knowing anything about it. If you've stayed away from vegetables all your life, it may just be because your mother cooked them to death and you never got to appreciate them in their true, well-prepared form. Or you may shy away from experimenting because you live with a partner or children who are culinarily challenged—that is, they won't eat it if they haven't eaten it before. But this is no reason to restrict your own taste buds! And sometimes, when those near and dear see you swooning over a new taste sensation, they may just take a nibble of what you find so delicious.

You may not be able to obtain certain foods at regular supermarkets, so you'll have to schedule a buying trip to a health food store or specialty shop. Here are some items that you may never have tasted:

Soy products (tempeh, miso, tofu, soy milk, soy nuts, soy burgers)

Tahini (a paste made of sesame seeds and oil used in many Mediterranean and Middle Eastern recipes)

Couscous (Moroccan grain, a nutty yellow accompaniment to lamb or vegetables)

Amaranth or quinoa (grains available in health food stores)

Shallots (like a more delicate cross between garlic and onion and great for flavoring other foods)

Unusual fruits such as star fruit (chewy, not too sweet—when you open it, the fruit forms a star shape) or

papayas—look around the fresh produce section, and
pick a fruit you've never tried before

Unusual vegetables such as artichokes, kohlrabies, or
dandelion or mustard greens—look around the fresh
produce section, and specifically pick a vegetable
you've never tried

Smoked salmon, or any smoked fish from the deli
department

If you want to go further, you can always browse through
the exciting pages of *The Visual Food Encyclopedia* (Macmillan). The
book will inspire you with suggestions for buying, cooking,
storing, and serving foods that are certainly not run-of-the-mill.
It contains such unusual edibles as cassava, ostrich fern, jicama,
and muskellunge.

You can take the legwork out of finding new foods by visit-
ing a restaurant for your innovative eating vacation. When din-
ing out, you might venture to try the following:

Nori (seaweed, used to wrap rice in Japanese sushi
preparation)

Quail eggs (used in Japanese sushi preparation, often
served raw)

Venison (highly seasoned, aged deer meat)

Ostrich (tastes like chicken, very low in cholesterol)

These treats will serve as a surprise to your mouth and will
make you a more adventurous person, ready to conquer new
worlds and open new avenues of pleasure.

64 ✷ The Chocolate Challenge

A sweet treat revives us. It's not just a surprise for the mouth but also an indulgence for the brain. This vacation will provide a taste sensation that you'll remember long afterward.

Studies have shown that the combination of sugar and fat is almost irresistible to most individuals. We go for cake, cookies, pie, ice cream, doughnuts, candy, and pastries with abandon. If we're bored or out of sorts, we may resort to the worst of all desserts—processed food loaded with chemicals.

But what kind of dessert would you really enjoy? What sweetness would linger in your mind long after the experience was over? If you can select a perfect candidate for your epicurean treat, you won't need much of it. One perfect chocolate, washed down with a perfect cup of tea, will do the trick.

It's a common experience to look for something to stave off hunger but mostly to stave off boredom. And once the sweet is eaten, it's forgotten. It's just a few more unwanted calories on your hips. But when we travel, we eat out a lot of the time, often sampling the finest of whatever the local cuisine has to offer. So, pretend you are in a foreign land, and go shopping for the exotic rather than the familiar.

Your vacation begins in the store, as you select your perfect treat. Chocolate is a serious matter for the chocoholic. There are many grades and flavors, from the bittersweet to the more mundane milk to the overlooked white. The best chocolate available is usually sold in a confectionery shop, but you can get some good imported chocolate in a supermarket if you have no specialty stores near you.

Look for Teucher first, everything else after that. (Other, more accessible brands that you might consider are Ghirardelli and Godiva.) All you need is one small piece for this trip. Chocolate has a lot of caffeine, and you don't need any more stimulation, so you're going to accompany your delicacy with a cup of herbal tea. Peruse the wide array of herbal teas now available. Pick something that won't stand out on its own. A lemon zinger might be nice, or even a peppermint tea. Loose tea is preferable to bagged.

When you've got your goods, set the kettle on. Put your one piece of chocolate on a beautiful plate, and get out your best cup and saucer. If you're making a pot of loose tea, put the leaves into a tea ball and pour boiling water over it, let the tea steep in the pot for at least ten minutes, then pour it into a cup (if it's too dark for you, add a little boiling water).

Take a bite of the chocolate, and let the delight of this experience wash over you. Is this the best thing you ever tasted? Your mouth will be filled with chocolate now, so it's time for a sip of tea to clear your palate. Wait before taking more chocolate: remember, you have only one small piece, and you want to make it last as long as possible. Life is like this, in many ways. The good stuff rushes by too fast, and we don't pay enough attention to it.

For now, in this vacation, we can savor the excellence, the comfort, and the absolutely divine flavor. As you finish your chocolate, congratulate yourself on your good taste and your restraint. You had only a little, but it was enough.

65 ✷ Potatoes à la Jackie O.

There are certain individuals who personify the word *classy*, and certainly Jacqueline Bouvier Kennedy Onassis was one of them. There was something about her style, her smile, her mysterious and rather shy presence, and her ability to get through the most harrowing of life's experiences that made her a woman we would all like to emulate. She could eat caviar off a spoon the way most people eat peanut butter.

Well, you may not have the Jackie O. look or her money, but you can do her potatoes just as well as she ever could. And as for the caviar, well, if you've got it, flaunt it, and if not, there's always the red lumpfish variety available in supermarkets.

This potato concoction, a kind of twice-baked potato with a little something extra, takes just a bit more time than regular baked potatoes and is definitely worth it. Your twenty minutes will be spent deconstructing and then reassembling the potatoes.

The potato is a lowly vegetable. As a matter of fact, a spud is often described as "the humble potato." It lives in the ground, and it's brown, covered with dirt and not particularly attractive. But Jackie O. was anything but humble, and her potatoes follow suit. This quick recipe raises the commoner of the vegetable world to mighty prince.

In order to take this twenty-minute gourmet trip, you need really good baking potatoes—not just any old thing that you might as well boil or fry as stick in the oven. Look for giant Idaho baking potatoes (they are sold loose but often come five to a bag), with no eyes or rooting knobs. Scrub them and puncture them with the tines of a fork in several places, or make a small slit in each side.

In the interest of time, you can microwave them, of course, but for real baked-potato texture, it's best to throw them in a 350° F oven for an hour. (This isn't eating up your twenty minutes, understand—you can do plenty of other things while your potatoes are baking the old-fashioned way.)

When they are done, slit the tops to let out the steam. With a spoon, scoop out the innards carefully, being sure not to break the skin. (If you mold and press the potato while you're scooping, you can break up the chunks of white filling, and it will come out more readily.) You will be left with a bowl of potato chunks ready for mashing and a few empty perfect skins. (Well, if you were Jackie O., they would be perfect; yours may be a little less than, but don't worry about it.)

Mash the white and add a healthy amount (you decide) of butter, cream or milk, salt, and pepper. If you want to be creative, you can add some fresh snipped chives or parsley, too. Some people like their mashed potatoes squashed completely; others like them with some lumps left in. I'll leave that part up to you.

Then, repack the potato skins with the potato mixture, and top with a healthy dab of beluga (pearly dark gray eggs), Sevruga (dark gray but not as fine as beluga), or Osietr (golden brown) caviar if you can afford it. If not, the lumpfish variety (red or black) will do just fine. Finish with a sprinkling of fresh snipped herbs and serve and eat.

66 ✷ Caribbean Delights

If you've ever had the good fortune to go to a Caribbean island resort, you'll recall the absolutely delicious fruit you can purchase at any roadside stand or restaurant. The mangoes, breadfruit, papayas, kiwis, and other wonderful fruits that comprise an important part of the diet of the islands grow abundantly along local roads, so it's easy to pick a juicy fruit right off the tree or vine. When you've consumed a few of these luscious treats, you're satisfied. You eat less because it tastes so good. And that's just what you'll do with your Caribbean Delights.

When we're feeling tense and anxious, we tend to dive into dessert or guiltily grab a candy bar to alleviate our craving for sweets. But an all-fruit meal will make you feel virtuous and good, and still satisfy your longing for sugar. Instead of stressing you out about the calories you're ingesting, Caribbean

Delights will calm you down and give you a needed boost. You'll also get a walloping serving of the healthful antioxidants vitamin C and beta-carotene when you tuck into this refreshment. (Beta-carotene is found in all fruits and vegetables with that great crimson or yellow orange color—flamingos have that incredible pink plumage thanks to all the shrimp they ingest— and you can get it from mangoes, papayas, sweet potatoes or yams, carrots, and squash, as well.)

Since we don't live on a Caribbean island, putting together an exotic all-fruit meal requires a trip to the supermarket. The next time you're up for a twenty-minute gourmet experience, purchase two ripe mangoes and two ripe kiwifruits (leave unripe ones sitting out or in a paper bag for at least three or four days until they are no longer hard). You'll also want a papaya and a few bananas. Most of your vacation will be spent peeling and cutting these fruits.

The mangoes first: remove the tough outer skin with a peeler or sharp knife, then cut in toward the hard white pit and take chunks off the mango. Understand that you will never get all the ripe fruit—mango pits are stubborn and cling to the fibrous bands—but that's all right. Be thankful you have at least a little mango.

Next, kiwis: try to make long, even peels to take off the fuzzy brown skin. When you are finished, you will be holding a beautiful green globe that you can slice into chunks.

Then the papaya: split the papaya in half, and scoop out the small black seeds in the center, then scoop the fruit from the rind.

Bananas are the easy part. Peel them, then cut one the long way to make a "boat," and the others into 1/4-inch slices.

Your meal will start with an appetizer of kiwi, served with a twist of lime. Then move onto your second course: a selection of mango, papaya, and banana chunks sitting in a banana boat. After all those sweet treats, you don't need dessert. Close your eyes, and you're in Aruba!

67 ✳ Colorful Cuisine

When you get hungry, do you think about the way food looks? Probably not—you're savoring the taste. On this vacation, however, you're going to think about color first, taste second. You can put together a meal that really stands out on the plate in just twenty minutes.

First, plan your menus. Let's imagine, for starters, an all-white meal. When you're thinking about white foods, you might come up with fish, turkey or chicken with no skin, white summer sausage, potatoes, mayonnaise, pasta or noodles, onions, water chestnuts, white bread, white sauce, yogurt, cream cheese or pot cheese, sour cream, white radishes, bulbs of scallions, leeks and fennel, and vanilla ice cream.

What about an all-red meal? When you're thinking about red foods, you might list beets or borscht, tomatoes, radishes, radicchio lettuce, red peppers, red chilis, red onion, red potatoes, roast beef or any other red meat, tuna tartare or sushi, red currant jelly, cherries, cranberries, red grapes, and plums.

As beverages, for your white meal, you would probably select milk or white wine (not actually white, but close enough), and tomato juice, fruit punch, or red wine for your red meal.

You could also plan a theme meal. If you're feeling patriotic, you could do a red, white, and blue presentation of roast beef and blue potatoes with sour cream. If you're thinking about Christmas, you might offer red kidney bean pie decorated with broccoli flowers, with a medley of red and green peppers on the side. A palette on your plate.

Eating for color certainly makes menu planning more interesting. Once you have your visual feast assembled, enjoy! Next week, you can switch colors and take another vacation.

68 ❖ One Bite at a Time

Food is wonderful. All those delicious flavors and great aromas make three meals a day worth waiting for. Of course, given the pace of life today, most of us rarely stop to savor what we consume. But using a well-known exercise, pioneered at the Stress Reduction Clinic at the University of Massachusetts Medical Center, you may find yourself relaxing around food and actually enjoying it more. In this vacation, you're going to take one bite at a time so that you can delight in the flavor, the texture, and the meaning of what you're putting into your mouth.

Above all, food is nourishment, a healing power in our lives. It's there to be enjoyed. But when we gulp down our meals and snacks without even tasting them, we miss out on so much. It's time to slow down and make eating fun again. Right now, in the next twenty minutes, you're going to learn how to fine-tune the way you eat so that you'll never have to diet again.

We're going to use a food that you don't ordinarily think much about: a raisin. Many people aren't that crazy about raisins, but give it a try. Remember, this is going to make great inroads in your attitudes about eating. A raisin works well in this exercise because it is hardly ever spotlighted in a meal. It's usually part of something else, such as raisin bread, or a muffin, or trail mix. People don't get attached to raisins, nor do they particularly adore them. So, you're now going to select one raisin from a box of them and get to know it better before you even think about eating it.

First, look at your raisin. Is it plump and juicy, or squashed flat? Is it round or oval or squared off? Can you imagine this raisin as the tender grape it used to be, before it was processed? See it lying in the sun, soaking up the rain. Now feel the various sides and planes of the raisin. Cover all its bumps and crannies. Rub it against your lower lip to feel the leathery texture.

Now it's time to taste the raisin. Lick it a little, to get a sense of its sweetness. Does it make you hungry? Even if you've recently had a meal, you have an instinctive understanding that you're about to eat, so you'll probably be salivating a little. Put the raisin in your mouth. Just roll it around so that you can experience the sensation and taste. How does it feel on your tongue, your teeth, your upper and lower gum ridges? The sweetness pervades your whole mouth now. Isn't it amazing how such a little piece of food has such a big effect?

OK, you can chew. Really chew. Masticate that raisin about thirty times. Chew on one side, then the other. Take tiny bites with your front teeth, too. Mash the raisin into pulp. The juice floods your consciousness. If you had any doubt as to what "raisin" tasted like, now you are fully aware of its various properties: the tang of it, the saltiness, as well as the sweet. It's small, but it gives you a lot to chew on, right?

When your raisin has nearly melted in your mouth, go ahead and swallow. What does it feel like to open and close your throat, to take that raisin inside you? The raisin is becoming part of you. You are heavier by one raisin, but you've burned calories in the process of consuming it.

In the few minutes remaining on your vacation, select another food—a heel of bread, a plum, a square of cheese—and consider it thoroughly before putting it in your mouth, chewing, and swallowing it. You don't have to take the time you took with the raisin now that you understand the principle. Practice this experience of mindful eating at your next meal, and see how much more delicious everything tastes. You'll eat less because each bite means more.

69 ✺ Spa Cuisine

You are what you eat. This catchy phrase that was so popular in the '60s is a little inaccurate: what's true is that you *become* what you eat. And if you take this vacation, in which you ingest foods that will stimulate your mind as well as your body, you may very well be better able to cope with the stresses of life.

Serotonin, a neurotransmitter or brain hormone, is one of the chemicals that the brain pumps out when we're enjoying ourselves, not feeling anxious, spending time with people we like. Tryptophan, a protein found in many foods, acts as a precursor to serotonin in the body—that is, the body can convert that substance into the feel-good neurotransmitter. When you eat a big turkey dinner and end up so relaxed that you can't stand up, well, it could be that you've eaten too much, but it may also have to do with the fact that turkey is loaded with tryptophan. A glass of warm milk before bed will produce the same result—a kind of soporific but delicious sense of peace and quiet inside.

On this vacation, then, you're going to make a meal of those foods that contain this good stuff. After all, when you take a trip, you want to eliminate hassles and just have a ball. That goes for eating as well as seeing the sights.

First, you must assemble the ingredients for feeling good. That means either buying a turkey and cooking it, or purchasing store-cooked brown-roasted turkey at the deli counter (don't buy the cheaper varieties which are full of preservatives). You'll also want a quart of milk. Some other serotonin boosters are bananas, mangoes, kiwis, fresh figs, plums, avocados, tomatoes, walnuts, and pecans. Select whatever your market has available.

When you return from shopping, put your meal on the table, and just contemplate it for a few minutes before delving in. Use the best plates you have, and don't cram too much food on one plate. You'll see an array of color and texture that is pleasing to the eye, certainly a part of the pleasure of eating. Make sure the milk is cold before you pour it (you can chill the glass first), and the turkey is either room temperature or warm. Slice the tomatoes and avocados for a salad. Put out a small dish of the nuts. Cut up the fruits for a fruit salad.

Now begin to consume your meal, eating slowly and relishing the mixture of flavors. After you've eaten half of what you consider a really good meal, stop for three minutes. Get up from the table and go do something else. Read a section of a magazine or book, look out the window, answer an E-mail message, or walk around the house. At the end of that time, see if you're still hungry.

If this vacation is helping you to relax and enjoy yourself, it will also inform your body as to how your mind feels. Appetite is a funny thing: there's a lag of about fifteen minutes between the time when an adequate amount of food has passed into the stomach and the time when the brain records it. The chemical messages traveling from the gut to the brain need that fifteen extra minutes to relay their information. During that quarter of an hour, you still feel hungry, even though you've eaten enough. And when you don't feel full, you generally eat more than you intend to. But when you're on a tryptophan diet, you may respond by feeling so good that you don't have to feel full.

If the tryptophan has started working, you may find that you are feeling satiated already—not stuffed or full, but as though you've eaten all you want. If not, fine; sit down and resume your meal. But have just a little more. When your mind and body are really in sync, you are able to reap the benefits of nourishment on a much deeper level.

70 ❧ Kneads and Wants

Back in the old days, you didn't get bread packaged and sliced. You made your own. And that's what you're going to do on this vacation. Bread is the most elemental of all foods—the "staff of life." A staff is a support; it holds you up. So if you have bread, you can survive.

"What?!" you'll exclaim. "You can't bake bread in twenty minutes." But in fact, that's about all the time required of you. The most interesting thing about bread is that it bakes itself as much as you bake it. That means that bread will do most of the job on its own, and all you have to do is make a few strategic moves. You are the catalyst; the bread is the active agent. The reason for this, of course, is the yeast or other rising agent (such as baking soda). Yeast is a living plant, sleeping until such time as warm water and sugar start the chemical reaction that releases its power. You do your thing, combining ingredients, and then the yeast goes to work and creates bread, which rises without any help from you. Your vacation can thus be spent really getting into the mechanism of how bread works, which is by punching down the risen dough and kneading it.

For a lovely white bread, start with the basics: dry active yeast (by the packet or square) and warm water. Put the yeast in a large bowl and add 3/4 cup of water; stir the mixture briefly, and let it sit until it becomes foamy. Now you're going to scald 3 cups of milk in a pan. Just turn up the heat so that the milk can come almost—but not quite—to a boil. When you see steam rising from it and the first few bubbles forming around the edge, take it off the heat. Then add 2 tablespoons of butter, 3 table-spoons of sugar, and 3 teaspoons of salt. Combine this with the foamy yeast, and start adding 8 to 9 cups of all-purpose flour. You've got enough when it all absorbs, with no little tidbits left on the side of the bowl.

Now it's time to knead. Kneading is great therapy because you can take out all your stresses, anxieties, and tensions on the bread. It is a satisfying pursuit, no matter how you are feeling, and appeals to every sense. First, there's the unmistakable aroma of bread dough. It smells wonderful. As soon as you start working your loaf, you get a whiff of that eternal warm yeast aroma that has sustained humans from time immemorial. Your mouth starts watering just considering what it will be like when you're done. Of course, the physical treat of pulling and pushing, molding, rolling, and shaping is considerable. What else gives in to your every demand and yet offers a bit of resistance? You can lose yourself in kneading as it becomes rhythmic, your whole body getting into the act. Your hands are filled with dough. They're involved in an activity like none other. They are creating something magnificent yet so simple that a child can do it.

Your vacation may be over when your kneading is done, but you can always pass the hat to someone else to finish the job— or take a double vacation if you like, since you get to do lots of other things during the times that your dough is rising. The next step is to shape the dough into a ball and place it in a buttered bowl, turning it around so that it's completely coated with a thin sheen of grease. Cover the bowl with a towel, and allow the dough to sit until doubled in volume (about an hour and a half). Punch the dough down—just listen to the extraordinary pop and sigh of the bread yielding to the impact of your fist—and allow it to rise again until doubled in volume (about a half hour to 45 minutes). Punch it down again, then split the ball in half, shaping each half into a ball. Put them on a board and cover them, allowing them to rise again for 10 or 15 minutes. Preheat the oven to 375° F. Grease two bread pans. Fold each mound of dough over lengthwise, and stretch it out to about three times as long as your pan. Fold each side into the center, and flatten the mounds into loaves. Place the loaves in the bread pans and bake for 55 minutes.

The glow on your face and on the faces of everyone who participates in this joyous event will be palpable. It's a whole other vacation just eating homemade bread!

8
Playing Games

Remember how great camp was? You could spend the whole day playing ball, swimming, hiking, or mastering the game of capture the flag. Your body was active and your mind floated free. Well, you're all grown up, but your spirit isn't.

On your mark, get set, *play!*

71 ❧ Ticktacktoe

Here is a great way to while away twenty minutes with a companion. You can use a piece of paper and a pen or pencil, or if you're outdoors, you can carve your game in the dirt with a twig.

Traditionally, you draw two vertical lines and two horizontal lines crossing them so that you create a box with nine spaces. One person takes the Xs, and the other takes the Os, alternating turns. The goal is to get three of your guys in a row across, down, or diagonally before your opponent does.

There are a couple of different styles to a successful game of ticktacktoe. Some people like to start out on the edges and work their way inside; others try to cram their markers on one side or another. Since games finish quickly, you can play a series of five when you're waiting for the family to get ready to go somewhere, or waiting with a colleague for a meeting to start.

If you want to give yourself and your partner more of a challenge, you can try the game with sixteen or even twenty-five squares instead of nine.

In order to use this game as a vacation, you must really throw yourself into it. Perhaps instead of lining up Xs and Os, you consider the game a means of releasing one problem at a time. Let your marker represent something that you've been chewing over, perhaps an unresolved problem or a person with whom you have a difficult relationship. Briefly give this issue your attention; then, as soon as you put your marker in a spot, let it go. When you have three problems stacked up in a row, congratulate yourself on your progress: you have succeeded in organizing them and arranging them so that you can deal with them later.

72 ✺ Gone Fishin'

It would be great to open your front door and find that you have a completely stocked trout pond, just waiting for you to fish in it. But as that's unlikely to occur in the near future, you can make do on this fishing vacation in which all you need is a stick or pencil, ruler or yardstick, a piece of string, safety pins, some paper "fish," and a paper clip you've pried open.

Use the first five minutes of your vacation to create ten "fish." You can simply tear bits of paper, then prebait them with a safety pin in the mouth of each one, and assign them points. Give the bigger fish more points, the smaller ones less. The total score should be 100. If you have different sizes of safety pins, you can also award higher points to the fish with smaller pins (since they'll be harder to snag).

Now make your fishing pole. Part of the fun of this game is creating the pole and line with whatever's available. Since you don't want to spend twenty minutes searching for special items, you might make do with a fork for the fishing rod and a rubber band for the line. If you've got a stick and string, so much the better. Tie the string to one end of the stick, and tie the open paper clip to the other end of your string as your hook.

Then there's the look of your fish. You can use odd scraps of paper, as noted, or you can go a little wild, cutting them into fish shapes. You can also label them—give them names like "new car," "dream vacation," or "new wardrobe"—and see what you reel in first.

Stock your pond by casting your fish into the water, which can be the rug in front of you or a bucket or pan. Time to go fishing! Your goal in the game is to earn 60 points in the first ten minutes, the rest in the next five.

Or, you can play it another way, which is fishing as mindful meditation. Forget the points, forget the score. Just spend a lazy twenty minutes trawling in the "water," enjoying the skill of snagging those big ones and throwing them right back. Think about the pleasure you can have, just flipping the rod and giving back what you've taken out.

73 ✷ Ghost in the Graveyard

This is a kid's game, similar to hide-and-seek. But it can be used by adults to provide a little adventure and excitement. You might play it late some afternoon after a killer day when you want a release before your various evening activities. You can play it with a group of friends, or recruit family members for the twenty-minute occasion.

It's best to play this game at twilight when the shadows are long and it's not so easy to see exactly where everyone is. The player who is "It" hides and everyone else counts to fifty at home base, which might be a large tree, the front porch, or the stoop. After the count, the players shout, "Ghost in the graveyard! Run, run, run!" They then start to move out in search of the "ghost," who at the same time is stalking them. The ghost tries to tag as many players as possible before they can escape, and then get back to home base. Anyone tagged becomes a ghost in the next round, where once again, players count to fifty at home base and then move out to find the old ghost and his or her new companions. Each successive round produces more ghosts, until finally, there is only one player—the winner—left "alive."

This game offers a way to feel both self-protective and vulnerable at the same time. You don't want to get caught, but on the other hand, it's fun to catch others. The falling darkness makes this a game that offers a sense of mystery and suspense, two elements that routine life often lacks. One way to get the most out of this activity is to use it as a conduit to that shadow world where our fantasies dwell. Being a "ghost" means you can step outside yourself and be the haunter, the one who gets others to hurry up and make decisions. When you're "alive" you want to take part in each moment; strive to be as much of a feeling, sensing person as you can be. If you can think of yourself as reaching for a goal, whichever role you're playing, you have a chance at turning this game into a real-life adventure.

74 ❖ Balancing Act

None of us feels that we have enough balance or harmony in our lives. We attempt to mix personal life and work, stress and relaxation, but usually end up feeling as if we are on one end of a seesaw, stuck up in the air or down on the ground, unable to move to center. On this vacation, therefore, you're going to learn how to achieve perfect balance by standing on one leg.

It doesn't seem hard, does it? Just lift one leg, and there you are on the other. But what do you have to do to keep the rest of your body perfectly still, to settle into the standing foot as though there were no tomorrow and you could stay there forever? It's a precarious perch for most of us. And that standing leg gets tired!

In order to gain good balance, start small. In the first five minutes of your trip, experiment on one foot, then the other, and see just how *out of balance* you can be. The moment before you're about to fall, relax completely. Maybe you *will* fall down—so what? The looser your limbs, the less it will hurt if you hit the floor. If you tense up, you'll lose it for sure. Now, as you're wavering there in space, do something, anything, to find your center again. You may have to wave your arms or bend your knee or bend over at the waist. The beginning of balance, then, is imbalance.

Now that you know it's possible to be tippy and then secure again, you're going to work on your body posture while you're on one foot. Stand in front of a mirror, and just lift your left foot up to the top of the toe, putting all your weight on your right foot. Your knee can be turned out or straight, but your standing foot should be turned out about forty-five degrees. Now lift that toe off the floor, and attach your left foot to your right ankle. Hold the posture. Stay like this as long as you can.

If you're getting tired, think about lifting up from the top of the thigh into the torso, as if all the muscles and tendons were being massaged upward. Don't lock your knee—leave it a little released. All you've done is to move the center of your body over to the center of your standing leg. Your leg is like a pedestal, supporting a beautiful vase or sculpture (the rest of your body).

The sculpture metaphor could inspire you to imitate actual works of art that you've seen. What about Rodin's *The Thinker*, or one of Degas's dancers? Switch sides. See if your balance has improved, or if this side is a little harder.

When you feel comfortable with your left leg on your right ankle, raise it higher, onto your knee. You can place your hands folded one over the other in the center of your chest. Breathe, and hold this posture. Don't you feel like a tree with roots that go way down into the ground, and leaves that extend up toward the sky? Beautiful!

In your final five minutes, play with the postures. Raise your clasped hands up over your head and stretch up from the sole of your foot to the ends of your fingertips. It's perfectly OK if you start feeling that you're getting out of balance. You can get right back again. Now take your left foot off your right knee and bring it behind you, grasping the toes with your left hand. Your knee should point straight down toward the ground. If you're flexible enough, you can reach back with your right hand and hold your foot with both hands. And if you're still comfortable, challenge yourself once more by leaning forward, focusing your gaze downward to give you a sense of direction. Repeat on the other side.

Gaining balance on your feet is directly related to gaining balance in life. When you know that no one can unsettle you, you can stride through your day with confidence and ease.

75 ❋ Jacks Be Nimble

Jacks is a very old game—a perfect vacation to take when you're anxious or distracted and you want something to do with your hands. All you need is five pebbles, which can usually be found if you walk outside and look around, or use five Tums or Tic Tacs.

First, practice. Squat down and place four of the stones on the ground in front of you. Place the fifth on the back of your hand. Flick your wrist, tossing the stone into the air, and while it's up there, pick up one stone from the ground before catching the one in the air. Next round, place one stone on the back of your wrist, flip it up, and pick up two stones before catching the airborne one. Repeat this until you can manage flipping and picking up all the stones. Soon you'll get the knack of throwing and scooping up, no matter how many you need to retrieve.

Now it's time to play. Start with all five stones on the back of your hand. Flip them up and catch them in your palm.

Next time, leave four stones on the ground, flip the fifth one, and pick up one before catching the one in the air. On the next throw, pick up the remaining three and catch the one in the air.

On the second round, pick up two stones with the first throw and two with the second, each time catching the one in the air.

On the third round, pick up one stone with the first throw and three with the second, each time catching the one in the air.

Finally, keep all four stones in your hand each time, and throw them down one at a time, two at a time, and so on, instead of picking them up.

If you find this vacation too simple—you never miss and never drop a stone—try it again with your eyes closed. See if you can feel what it's like to throw gently, right in front of your face, and sense the slight rush of air as the stone goes past you. You'll probably miss them all—even if you use your second hand to swipe the ground and let the first hand catch. It doesn't matter whether you get them or lose them. Don't get stressed. Hey, it's your vacation, remember?

The sense of sight is a wonderful thing, but an inner vision will allow you to imagine the stones in the air and on the

ground; you can feel them in your hand. These three locations
are connected. And as you become better able to visualize the
stones flipping up and landing exactly where you want them,
you will find your hand reaching at just the right moment in just
the right place.

You might become a champion of a new type of game, one
in which the goal is not to win anything, but to discover the
infinitely powerful potential of not wanting, not doing, not car-
ing so much.

76 ❧ Jump!

Jump rope is one of the best types of exercise around. It's also
a great game to play when you're antsy and need a physical
break. You can use a cotton, nylon, or polypropylene rope with
handles. You'll know it's the right length by placing one foot
in the center of the rope and drawing up the two sides with
your arms. The handles should just reach your armpits. When
you jump, wear athletic shoes or sneakers that can take some
impact.

Warm up a little before you start jumping by doing shoulders rolls and ankle rolls. Work on alternate hopping—one foot
comes off the ground, then the other—and jumps, in which both
feet jump and hit the floor together. Jump on the balls of your
feet. Think light, like a cat coming down on its paws as it grace-
fully leaves a piece of furniture, heading for the floor. You
should feel bouncy, like a rubber ball.

It's time to add the rope. First, practice swinging the rope
in a circle beside your body as you jump in place. This way, you
don't have to coordinate feet and arms. The most common
jump-rope pattern begins with you holding the rope behind
you, turning it counterclockwise. Hold both handles in your
right hand. As you jump, make a circle from back to front with

your right arm, and let the rope hit the floor when your feet are up in the air. Then repeat on the left side.

Now you're ready to put the whole thing together. Holding one handle in each hand, place the rope behind you so that the center of the rope touches the backs of your heels. Turn the rope over your head, your arms circling inward, and scoot it under your feet, jumping lightly as it hits the surface. Keep the rope moving—your arms should never stop. Jump on one foot at a time, then switch to both feet.

If you're swinging away and never missing, you can reverse the rope, letting it swing from front to back. Again, go back to your practice exercises. Hold the rope in your right hand, and begin to make backward or clockwise circles on each side as you jump in place. When you've mastered that, go on to regular jump rope, this time with your arms circling outward.

Here are some classic jump rope rhymes. You won't be able to memorize them in your allotted twenty minutes, so photocopy the pages from this book and tape it to a wall right in front of your jumping spot so that you can read it. You'll find that the rhythm of the words helps your jumping, and the rhythm of the jumping helps you to remember the words after you've done it a few times.

> *Miss Susie had a steamboat*
> *The steamboat had a bell*
> *Miss Susie went to heaven*
> *The steamboat went to*
> *Hello operator, give me number nine*
> *And if you disconnect me*
> *I'll kick your big be-*
> *Hind the 'frigerator, there was a piece of glass*
> *Miss Susie sat upon it and cut her little*
> *Ask me no more questions*
> *Tell me no more lies*

The boys are in the girls' room pulling down their
Flies are in the meadow
The bees are in the park
Miss Susie and her boyfriend
Are kissing in the
D-A-R-K, D-A-R-K, D-A-R-K
[fast] DARK! DARK! DARK!
Dark is like a movie
A movie's like a show
A show is like a TV screen
And that is all I know
I know I know my mother
I know I know my pa
I know I know my sister
With the eighty-acre bra!

The following rhyme is one that most everyone knows:

Lincoln, Lincoln
I've been thinkin'
What the heck
Have you been drinkin'?
Looks like water
Tastes like wine
Oh, my gosh
It's turpentine!

And here's a third:

Down in the meadow where the green grass grows
Sat little [name of jumper], sniffin' at a rose.
She sang so high and she sang so sweet
That along came [2nd name] and kissed her on the cheek.

He kissed her on the cheek, and he kissed her once again.
She wanted him to stop, but she couldn't say just when.
Then along came [3rd name], a big, strong lout,
And without a single word, he pushed [2nd name] out!

77 ✭ Zen Handball

Kids on the street love handball. They don't need anything
except a Spaldeen and a wall. They'll wham that little thing over
and over, getting out all sorts of aggression, enjoying the sound
of skin hitting rubber. The object in traditional handball is to hit
the ball at the wall with your hand in such a way that your
opponent can't return it. But if you haven't got an opponent, and
you are playing against yourself, relax. In Zen handball, you
have no intention to hit the ball again. You may, and then you
may not. The point of the game is to see what happens.

Begin the game by marking your territory. You may be in a
playground or perhaps against the garage in your backyard. Your
playing field is a rectangle: the wall marks one of the short sides.
(Most courts are twenty feet by thirty-four feet, but if you have
less space, so be it.) Designate a serving line parallel to the wall,
about sixteen feet in front of it.

Now drop the ball and bounce it a little. Test its resilience
and its possibilities. Sometimes just a gentle tap from your hand
can send it skyward; at other times, you have to come down
hard just to get a decent bounce out of it. This is mainly because
of the angle of your hand and the amount of "cup" in your palm.

Now try serving. Bounce the ball in front of you, pull back
your right hand and smack that ball at the wall. It must hit in
front of the serving line in order to score. The wall now
becomes your partner. Watch the trajectory of the ball as it

returns to you. It may come flying back, go over your head, or hit just short of you. Or, it may hit the wall at a strange angle and pop up, then dribble down to the ground.

Run up and stroke the ball back toward the wall—you don't have to wait for it to bounce. On the other hand, you can let it bounce several times. In regular handball, you have only one chance: if the ball bounces more than once and you don't hit it, you lose points. But in Zen handball, it's fine to let the ball bounce. In this version, you want to summon the ball to come to you, which it just might do if allowed to take its own sweet time. There is nothing as satisfying as a ball that owes its allegiance to you and seems to direct itself, like a homing pigeon, right back to your hand.

Of course, if it's about to die on the vine, you'll want to go up and give it another tap to start the cycle over again. Don't forget that you can use either hand in this endeavor, and you can take any number of steps to reach your goal. But don't hurry; don't get yourself into a lather over this. Be content to allow the ball to do what it wants.

Enjoy the experiment, and see whether your game improves as you calm down, deal with the ball, and deal with yourself in a playful way. This is a vacation first and foremost, and the goal is to have fun.

78 ✱ License Plate Poker

Here's a wonderful way to spend twenty minutes when traffic is slow and you're clearly not going to make your meeting on time. You can play alone as you sit in the driver's seat, or with a few companions. You're going to identify license plates that will give you a great poker hand. You'll simply use the letters on the license plates of cars you see to put a winning combination together.

The best plates contain the letters J, Q, K, or A, which stand for "jack," "queen," "king," and "ace." The rest of your hand will come from the numbers—higher numbers trump lower ones. Let's say you see a car with the plate BAM 98G: you have an ace, a 9, and an 8. If your companion sees ZQA 224 (a queen, an ace, and a pair), that hand beats yours. Since there aren't any suits in the game (no clubs, hearts, spades, or diamonds), you make your good hand with pairs, or three or four of a kind. Straight flushes (a sequence of the five highest cards of a suit) are very rare, but one day you might just run into the license plate KQA 10J. That would be something for the record books!

79 ❦ Kick the Can

Are there days when you just want to haul off and kick something—or someone? Why not put your rage aside, or at least turn it into a fun-loving game? Kick the can is a wonderful way to blow off steam.

You'll need a can (or ball, but a can makes more noise). Put it on a particular site that you designate as home base—right next to a tree or rock, for example. One player is "It," and the remaining players are free agents.

The person who is "It" kicks the can as far away as possible from home base while the others run and hide. "It" then retrieves the can, places it next to home base, and counts to fifty. "It" then announces, "Ready or not, here I come!" and starts looking for the other players. When a player is spotted, "It" runs home, bangs the can, and shouts, "Kick the can—one, two, three!" The exposed player is considered captured and has to return to home base.

The captive is temporarily out of the game until the other players have been found. A hiding player can release a captured player by coming up and kicking the can away from home while

"It" is out hunting for others, but this works only if you have many players. As soon as the can is off home base, all the captured players are free, and "It" has to go retrieve the can and start retaking prisoners.

When "It" has brought everyone home, the first player captured then becomes "It," and a new round begins.

The farther you go, the better you hide, and the longer the game lasts. But for even twenty minutes, it's a lot of fun.

80 ❧ Ultimate Frisbee

Whoever invented the Frisbee was some kind of genius. It flies like a kite, it has heft like a ball, and it's even easy for dogs to catch because it has a nice lip that fits between two of theirs. Watching a Frisbee sail through the air is so satisfying that tossing one back and forth is a great way to spend a twenty minute vacation.

But because it's boring to play catch all the time, you're going to turn this trip into a tournament. You can play with any number of throwers greater than two. First, set up your field, with side boundaries, a centerline, and goals at both ends. One teammate from each side stands behind each goal, waiting to catch the Frisbee thrown by his or her side. (If there are only two of you, forget the goalies and just throw over the line.) No one is allowed to run or walk with the Frisbee—only pivoting is allowed.

Side A starts by throwing over the centerline toward side B. If the B players fail to catch it, the A team rushes forward, passing the Frisbee from teammate to teammate until it reaches the goal line. Passes can be intercepted by the opposing team, who will then begin to throw the Frisbee back toward their goal. A foul is a pass that ends up beyond the side boundaries; a player of the opposite team then retrieves the Frisbee and throws it back into play. The team with the highest score at the end of twenty minutes wins.

If you have no companions, you can still take a Frisbee vacation. Give yourself challenges such as distance throwing (see if you can sail it past a certain point), target shooting (see if you can hit a target thirty or forty feet away from you), or one-finger catches (see if you can throw the Frisbee in the air, then run and catch it on one finger).

You may have so much fun on this vacation that you'll start packing a Frisbee in your attaché case along with your lunch. Happy throwing!

81 ❧ ESP

The powers of the mind are extraordinary, and we hardly use them at all in our everyday life. On this vacation, you are going to leave your left brain behind and work with your right brain on the powers of intuition.

Think about the times that you had an inkling of something about to happen and didn't act on it—or did act on it, and felt weird for days afterward because you couldn't begin to imagine where you got your information. There is no way to prove that we can predict the future or fathom what another person is thinking, but the more we experiment with our dormant powers, the better we tend to get. Some people are naturals—their awareness appears to be deeper and fuller than those of normal mortals. But the skills necessary to peer through the veil of consciousness can be honed. That's what you're going to do on this trip.

You can use an ordinary deck of cards to get started. You'll also need some paper and a pen or pencil. First, take a few deep breaths, and calm yourself internally and externally. Shuffle the cards, and think seriously about the numbers and suits passing through your hands. Imagine a liquid line of colors flashing from one hand to the other. Pat the deck neatly and place it face down in front of you.

Lay your hand on the top of the deck, and close your eyes. Think about seeing through the top of each card, actually peeling off the backing so that you can visualize the exact color, the suit, and the number or picture on the card. For now, you're going to work with just one parameter. There are only two colors, so let's start there. You have a 50 percent chance of being right.

You aren't going to guess. You are going to *see* the card. Know without doubt that it is either red or black. Write down your assumption, then place that card to one side, and work on the next card. Continue until you have ten cards beside you and ten colors recorded on your pad. Compare the two. How well did you do? If your average is better than 50 percent, it's time to go on to suits.

Here you have a one-in-four chance of being right. Once again, try ten cards, and write down ten assumptions. If you're doing brilliantly, you can try for numbers or the faces on the face cards. And finally, think about the whole card, and put all these elements together. It's possible that the next card down will in fact be what you've said it is.

Now can you reverse the procedure? Clairvoyants can trick time and say that something is about to happen before it does. For this round, place your hand on the deck, and splay it out face down in front of you. Say aloud the designation of a certain card: "The next card I touch will be red," or "This card will be a club." Then let your hand fall on the card that just feels right. Once you get good at this, you can try for the whole picture: "This card is the jack of hearts," or "the two of spades."

Although demonstrations of ESP and clairvoyance are often thought of as party games, they are quite serious. We think of the world as a concrete place, accessible only by our five senses. But our sixth sense, intuition, is also responsible for the way we perceive the world. How do we know not to get on a certain flight? Why are we anxious when the phone rings on one particular occasion and not others? It's because something deep in our subconscious sparks just for a minute and tunes us in to a perspective on the world that we can't usually imagine. The more we give this sense range and credence, the more we'll be able to use it when we need it.

Keep taking those trips to the land of ESP. You never know what you may find there.

82 ❈ Punch and Judy

It is not politically correct to want to hit, punch, bite, or pummel, but sometimes, you simply have to let all that stored-up tension out of your system. This vacation is a physical one similar to paintball in which you stalk an opponent through the woods and shoot gobs of paint at the person as though you were in a real war situation. Punch and Judy is a little tamer: there's no opponent except the demons inside you, and you take out your aggressions on a couch or punching bag.

When my daughter was a toddler and cursed with the Terrible Twos, the best thing I purchased for her was a plastic blowup rendition of Peter Pan's Captain Hook. The toy was just a little taller than she was, with a weighted bottom. In her moments of mounting frustration and anger, I would direct her toward the Captain with an encouraging, "Let 'im have it!" and she would then whale away at the toy while it bobbed and ducked under the onslaught. It was great therapy! She would yell, scream, and kick, and end up exhausted, having blown out all the rage and anger inside her. For the rest of the evening at least, she would be a sunny child with a great disposition.

You, too, can take the edge off. All you need is a plastic bat, a couch or bed, and a punching bag (either the standing or mounted variety) or pillow. Adults, of course, don't have the abandon of kids, and it will be hard at first to express your feelings. But in this game, there are no limits.

Start with a little warm-up. Bend your knees and swing your arms back and forth, bringing them up a little higher with each swing. Now swing them across your body. Make a light fist, and jab the air in front of you. You will find that as you begin, the spirit of the game will grab you. You'll soon be into your footwork, determined to get your revenge on whoever it is that's bothering you.

If you have a bat, this is the time to pick it up. Feel its heft; test its strength. If someone pitched you a ball right now, you could hit it out of the park. Instead, take that bat to the nearest couch and start to pound. Listen to the satisfying *thwack* as it makes contact with a padded surface. Feel the rhythm of your body as it moves the bat into position, then allows gravity (and a little muscle power) to take it smack down into the couch.

Start working the punching bag or pillow with little taps— one hand and then the other. Accelerate in speed and strength, and see if you can get the thing to fly back and forth. It's OK to make noise—encouraged, even! Let out a yell when you make contact. Getting the grief and rage out is part of this trip, and the more you say yes to the experience of acting aggressive in a controlled setting, the more you'll feel that you have taken charge of your troubles.

As you approach the end of your trip, start to slow down. Let your breathing return to normal. Compare the way you felt before you began with the way you feel now. Have you chased the "wild things" out of your system? Do you feel ready to meet the world? Are you a little more in tune with the people around you?

It's not considered nice to feel hostile toward anyone or anything, but sometimes it's unavoidable. Don't feel guilty about this journey. Take it as a gift, a way out of a sticky situation. When you're in the throes of fury, that is when you start on the road back to peace and sanity. It's the people who don't let it out who are dangerous!

9
Arts & Crafts

You may not be able to spend the day splattering paint like Pollock, and you probably don't have time to retreat to a quilter's colony for a month, but there are other, quicker ways to get your juices flowing. Let your creative side break free!

83 ❧ Sail into the Sunset

A cruise on a yacht can be the most luxurious of all vacation possibilities. Your hand on the tiller, champagne before dinner, and a cozy cabin below deck. But who do you know with a yacht who'd be willing to take you along?

The solution, of course, is making a boat of your very own. Suppose you could construct the perfect boat in less than twenty minutes, one that would be ready to sail faster than you can say "origami"? That's what you'll do on this exciting trip.

Origami, a Japanese word that literally means "to fold paper," started in China about the first century A.D. In the sixth century, Buddhist monks introduced the art of making paper to Japan, and paper became a major influence in Japanese culture. (The word for paper, *kami*, is a homonym for the word for "spirit" or "god.") The practice of folding beautiful paper into intricate designs was a female tradition, passed on from mother to daughter.

You can use any stock at all—from copier paper to newsprint to fancy laminated papers that have a shiny texture and, often, one color on the surface and a different color on the back. If you get into origami in a big way, you'll want to visit the many websites that open the magic world of paper to those in the know. For starters, try Joseph Wu's Origami Page at www.origami.vancouver.bc.ca/.

In order to make your sailboat (which actually floats), all you need is a sheet of rectangular paper from your copier or

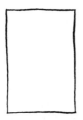

1. Start with one piece of rectangular paper.

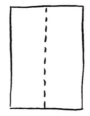

2. Fold in half the short way.

3. Crease (fold and unfold) down the middle.

4. Fold top corners down to the center crease.

5. Fold top layer only of the bottom edge up as far as it will go.

6. Turn over and repeat step 5 on the other side.

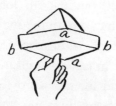

7. Reach inside and pull the front and back away from each other.

8. Continue pulling until the two A corners are folds and the two B corner are flat.

9. Tuck one end of the brim under the other; do the same at the other point. Now it will lie flat.

10. Fold bottom point to top. Fold only the top layer.

11. Turn model over and repeat on the other side.

12. The result.

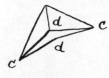

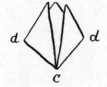

13. Repeat steps 7 and 8, squashing C corners together until they touch.

14. Fold and unfold to make a crease. Fold only the top layer. Turn over and repeat on back.

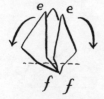

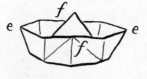

15. Pull the tow E corners apart. F corners will be drawn upward to the top of the model.

16. The complete sailboat.

loose-leaf notebook. The stiffer the paper, the harder it is to fold, but the more durable your boat will be and, thus, the longer you'll sail it. The following fifteen-step sailboat, courtesy of Valerie Kull, a particularly talented origami aficionado, will have you crowing with delight at your paper-folding success in just a few easy minutes. And if you are all thumbs and get too frustrated to finish the project, you can use a sheet of newspaper and stop at drawing number 7 to make a party hat. Put it on and celebrate!

84 ✻ Drawing from Memory

Are you a natural artist? Or can you barely create a stick figure? Whatever your level of talent, you'll enjoy this excursion into drawing on the right side of the brain, where you explore the potential of the creative, intuitive part of yourself.

Most of us examine and organize everything. We make lists, we come up with concrete plans, and we file according to topic. That's what our jobs require of us, so we've become expert in those analytic areas. We rely primarily on left-brain skills, and we function well in typical situations by thinking clearly and carefully, following directions, and moving from point A to point B by the shortest distance.

Every once in a while, it's helpful to take a break from ordinary left-brain activity and let the right brain come to the fore. When you allow your pencil to move across the page without thinking about how to achieve a certain goal, you are freeing up the fluid potential of your creative spirit.

Let's say you'd like to draw a cat. You know that a cat has a head with two eyes, a nose, and a mouth; a body; four paws; ears that stick up; whiskers; and a tail. To draw a cat from memory takes a certain feeling for perspective, proportion, and quality of line (how do you draw fur, anyway?). Using a sleeping cat as a model may make your task even harder, since you need to see and then recreate as you alternately observe your model and then your drawing.

But suppose you approach drawing in a completely different way. Suppose you forget about form and function and just think movement and line. Forget that you have any idea whatsoever that you know intrinsically what a cat looks like.

On this vacation, you are going to copy a drawing that you particularly like. Don't worry about how hard that seems: you can do it! For your first artistic vacation, however, it's best to select a rather simple drawing, something like a greeting-card version of a cat. After you've shown yourself what a talented sketcher you are, you can move on to a Monet or Picasso rendering of a cat.

In addition to the painting or drawing that you will be copying, you'll need a sketchpad or blank sheet of paper and a sharpened pencil with an eraser. The first step is to turn your model upside down. That's right! Flip it over.

Take the first couple of minutes to look—really look—at the group of lines, dots, and dashes in front of you. This isn't a cat anymore, but rather, just a sequence of marks on paper. Since you no longer have to draw a familiar image, the pressure is off. You are no longer trying to make sure that the cat's face is in proportion with her ears; all you have to do is copy the lines and squiggles on the drawing. Much easier!

Divide your drawing into three sections—a top, middle, and bottom—and cover the sections you're not yet working on. Begin by copying the lines and marks that you see at the top of the page. All you need concern yourself with is the distance from one line to the other and where those lines sit in relation to the sides of your paper. Your left brain will tell you that you're copying a set of upside-down cat's paws, but obliterate that thought from your head. All you have to do is mark the various lines on your paper. When you finish your first section, cover it and move to the middle of the drawing; when you complete that cover it, and finish with the bottom of the drawing. Make sure you get in as many squiggles, blobs, and doodads as you see. An accurate eye is important here.

Now invert your masterpiece. You will be amazed to note that you have drawn a cat. Does it resemble the original? What's different about it? Where could you improve on it? You can use your eraser to fix any egregious errors, but give yourself credit for seeing well and for allowing your right brain to fly.

If you enjoyed your trip and are proud of it, spend the last five minutes hanging your drawing on the wall—or at least the refrigerator—for all to see.

85 ❧ Walking the Labyrinth

The original labyrinth was no vacation. King Minos in Ancient Greece constructed it to house the Minotaur, a terrible beast, half man and half bull, who ate nine young men and nine young women each year. But the labyrinth you will walk on this journey will offer you a quiet haven, a meditative start or end to your busy day.

The concept of the labyrinth is a spiraling path that always leads inward. (It should not be confused with a maze, which has a lot of false starts and blind alleys.) When you begin walking your labyrinth, you may think of Dorothy, starting along the yellow brick road to Oz. Or you may think of your own personal journey as you make your way through life. Finding your way in is also finding your way out, because they are the same.

As in life, we move forward slowly, taking one step at a time. We don't necessarily have to know where we're going—the fact that we're going is the only thing that counts.

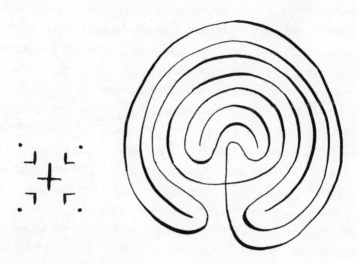

The seven-circuit labyrinth diagram.

For this vacation, you'll need a piece of sidewalk chalk and the seven-circuit diagram shown here as a model. The seven rings make up the classic labyrinth design. Seven, of course, is a number that comes up frequently in numerology—from the number of days in the week to the belief that seven augurs good luck.

Use the first figure to get the center of your labyrinth. You'll note that it looks like a cross, but you're going to draw it with curves rather than straight angles. Now use the second figure to extend the arcs of your circle outward from these initial points. Continue the arcs until they spiral around seven times, just like the second figure.

After spending the first ten minutes drawing your labyrinth, spend the second ten minutes mentally walking it. Start at the opening on the left side of the cross. Try putting yourself in different places in the labyrinth, and find your way out. Walk it backward, taking measured steps. Be silent as you move around this figure. Stay in the present moment. Take measured steps, slowly and carefully. Try to think of the activity in which you're engaged, rather than allowing your thoughts to skip outside the confines of the labyrinth. You are taking a trip to the center of yourself and back out again, and you cannot hurry the process. Simply allow it to happen and you will find that each time you travel to this site, you will instantly calm down and embrace the journey ahead.

86 ∗ The Fall Collection

There is no more spectacular sight than a hill full of New England maples in October. The crimsons, yellows, oranges, browns, and greens are a riot of color on the landscape. If you'd like to have the benefit of this beauty all year long, you can make a leaf press and keep what you love under glass.

All you need is a picture frame. Any size will do, but obviously, the larger the surface, the more room you'll have inside to display your treasures. Pick a lovely autumn day, and get yourself to a street or park where the leaves are falling. This is nature in all her glory. What a refreshing change from the manufactured world in which most of us live most of the time.

Take a full ten minutes to hunt around for the best specimens. You can pick up multicolor leaves, berries, roots, twigs, soft beanlike pods, or bits of moss. (Acorns are too hard and won't squeeze into the frame, but you might be lucky and find a broken one that's been flattened.) Select what is pleasing to your eye and will offer the most variety. You'll find, as you go, that you are attracted to certain items and not others. Do you like leaves that look similar or different? Are you drawn by an irregular shape or a symmetrical one? You can tell a lot about your personality simply by examining the types of things you select.

Once you've collected your treasures, carry them back inside and assemble them in a row so that you can survey the bounty.

Open your frame and lay the cardboard down in front of you.
Then start your collage. You may want to keep your background
neutral, or you may decide to cover the cardboard with a piece
of wrapping paper, sheet music, or a poem. Something that has
special meaning to you will enhance your project.

Now start to position your leaves and woodsy collectibles.
Don't think too much about making a pattern. It's better to
allow yourself to take this vacation with your hands and see
how creative they can be. You can layer one leaf on another, and
throw down a spray of berries in the middle. You can lay down
a root and let a twig seem to grow out of it. You can keep the
distribution of things even, or bunch them up in one corner or
the center. Don't feel that you have to fill the entire frame; it's
pleasing to the eye to leave some blank space.

Try not to correct yourself. This is an intuitive piece of art-
work using only the elements of the earth, and Mother Nature
herself makes plenty of mistakes. Just place your items where
they make aesthetic sense. Then position the glass over the
cardboard, and flip the entire assembly over. Press down
firmly—this will squash any berries or pods you've got—and put
the clamps in place.

Turn your masterpiece over to see what you've created.
That autumn day is now yours forever, a vacation to remember.

87 ❧ Squeezing the Most Out of Life

When you were a kid, or when you had young kids, you could
revel in the satisfying sensation of digging your hands into clay
or Play-Doh. It has an undeniable presence: it's a mass that you
can move and shape to your own devices. You don't have to be
a great artist to work with Play-Doh; all you have to be is ready
and willing to dig in and make something. In our everyday lives,
we spend far too much time thinking about things or asking

other people to create things that we can use. This vacation takes you back to your roots.

Right now, you're going to return to those glorious days of yesteryear, when you could feel that you were really constructing objects that were all your own—even if you can't identify them.

A trip to a toy store will give you all the Play-Doh you need. (You can make it at home, although it takes more than twenty minutes, and the quality of the home-cooked variety usually isn't as fine as the manufactured.) Because the dough comes in colors, you can play around with mixing and matching. Why not a blue dog with a yellow head?

Remove any rings you might be wearing, and begin. For the first few minutes, just get the feel of the stuff. Roll it, knead it, bang it flat, and throw it on the floor. Close your eyes, and become aware of that unmistakable odor, the Play-Doh smell you remember from childhood. As soon as the stuff softens in your warm hands, the aroma will become even more noticeable. Do you like it or hate it? Can you make this sensual trip back to the past a part of this vacation?

Now get into the tactile element of using the material to make shapes. Be sure your whole hand stays active. Use your fingers, palms, the heels and backs of your hands. Make long loops and pinch them together; make round balls of different sizes and stack them on top of each other. See how many different objects you can make, and decide whether you like working in miniature or as large as you can. Enjoy the sensation of watching your hands at work. Although this is a vacation, it's one in which you test different types of potential that you may have and never use.

For the next ten minutes, see what you can do with the shapes you've already made. Flatten out a large circle into an oval, and put a few small circles into it to make a face. Use the looped strands to make hair. Now elaborate on it and add expression: is it sad, angry, happy? Break off pieces, and change your vision of what a face should be.

Don't feel that your first attempt must be carved in stone. Yes, you can bake your creation and keep it just as you made it, or you can return it to the void. As a matter of fact, one of the nicest things about this experience is that your work is always flexible and elastic. You can simply collapse your creation, separate out the different colors, and allow the raw materials to sit in front of you once again, ready to receive a new shape and form. This will teach you not to attach great importance to anything you do and to see how life, just like Play-Doh, is in constant flux.

When you play with Play-Doh, you are tapping into the part of yourself that once dared to make mud pies and roll down hills. On this vacation, you can explore the depths of your creativity and your lack of permanence.

88 ✷ Bubblicious

On the worst of days, bubbles revive you. There's something funny and beautiful about a translucent bubble, and for twenty minutes, it's definitely worthwhile allowing a stream of them into your life.

You may say that blowing bubbles is not an art or a craft; I say it is both. It is an art to manipulate the soap and water so as to give you the best bubbles, and it is a craft that vanishes as soon as you've constructed it. One of the best things about this vacation is that it is immediate: you get what you want out of it and then it's over with. No compromises, no regrets.

You can make your own soap mixture. A squeeze of Ivory liquid into a quart of water will do it. Or you can purchase a bubble set (liquid and wand) at a toy store or bed and bath store. You have probably also seen the variety of wands that range in size from a dime to large enough to stick your head through—they can be lots of fun too.

Take your liquid and wand outside, and spend a few minutes experimenting with some trial bubbles. If you blow hard and fast, you'll get a tiny product that is gone as soon as it arrives. If you blow slowly and steadily, you'll create a bubble of considerable size that sticks around a little while. Try waving the wand instead of blowing on it, you'll get a stream as long as your arm if your movement is continuous. Now dip your wand, and then start running forward. As you look back, you'll be leaving a trail that pops and bounces behind you.

Once you have the knack of bubble making, you're ready to take a real trip. Figure out what you'd like out of it before you launch into it. Do you want to be surrounded by bubbles at all times? Then, you'll have to keep blowing or keep moving your arm. Are you content with an occasional bubble? Then, work slowly to expand one bubble in your wand. As you suck the air in and out, you'll see the bubble shimmering in its frame before it finally lets go and starts drifting away. Blow more quickly and see how many you can keep in the air at one time.

Spend your vacation trying to get the best, rather than the most, out of your bubble experience. Let a bubble rise and catch it on your wrist or shoulder. Feel the wetness of its touch. Look carefully at a bubble and admire the transparent rainbow inside it. It is so delicate, yet so strong. What can you see inside the bubble? Can you imagine yourself entering the shelter of the bubble and being kept safe from all harm? As you start to see the strength in this lighter-than-air apparition, you'll recognize the integrity and brilliance, the light and shadow, of this pocket of air. As with most vacations, now you see it; now you don't.

89 ❧ Handy Creations

Most of the time, we are rewarded for keeping things neat and tidy, from our desks to our love lives. But every once in a while, it's a good idea to make a mess. Finger painting can be a terrific release when you're stressed out. Be willing to dive in and get creative.

For this escape you'll need some finger paints in various colors and some fairly heavy drawing paper. A smock is a good idea if you have to get right back to the office or you have an appointment where you're expected to look like a grown-up. Roll up your sleeves, remove your rings, and you're ready to go.

Open the jars of paint, and sniff them. This should call up memories of childhood, a rainy day when your mom lined the kitchen floor with brown paper and told you not to bother her until you'd created a masterpiece. The heady smell of the colors is an invitation, asking you into the world of art. You don't need a plan or an idea. Just get busy dipping your fingers in.

The feel of the paint should also be a tantalizing experience. We're used to the textures of face cream and petroleum jelly—the mundane—but for a tactile rush, there's nothing like the greasy, cool, velvety feel of paint. Rub it around in your fingers, smear a little on the paper in front of you. Make a handprint; see how your hand looks after it's been coated in blue, green, or yellow.

What's it like to mix colors? On this vacation, you want to feel as free as a child, and as insightful as Jackson Pollock. (You, also, can throw the paint onto your canvas, but put a drop cloth against the wall if you're going a little nuts.) Work a smear of red into the blue to make purple; add a dash of yellow to blue to create green—maybe even a little red to make forest green—then add more yellow and get several lighter shades.

Think shape. Do you want to be representational and do your own version of a cave painting, or do you want to play with abstract art? If you want bold strokes, use the palm or heel of your hands; for lightly etched places, use your fingernails. It's fun to scratch a new color into a wash of another.

Sit back and admire your work. Of course, you can't do much in fifteen minutes, but your sketch will give you a sense of your potential. That's what a vacation should do—just open some doors that have been closed for a long time.

For the last five minutes, clean up. See what amazing color you get as the water rinses your hands. But even after your blue-green-orange-red-black hands turn their natural color again, you're sure to have a little remnant left under the nails.

This will serve to remind you, during that boring board meeting, where your real creativity lies.

90 ✿ Cut Out for Some Fun

Here's a little trip to take when people are hassling you and you can't stand the pressure another minute. You're going to create an exotic and sophisticated set of paper pals, complete with costumes, to protect and support you.

Paper dolls were popular in the nineteenth century as a way to show off designs that were intended for dress patterns. A dressmaker would cut out a basic model and then do a practice version of an ensemble, complete with hat, gloves, purse, and other accessories. The clothing would be attached to the doll by means of paper tabs that folded around the figure. In addition to having a miniature replica of the costume to come, the dressmaker had a toy for the children to play with.

At some point, the dolls became more amusing than the clothing they wore, and people started pleating the paper to connect the figures for added dimension. Children could make these themselves.

And so can you, in less than twenty minutes. The technique of cutting paper dolls requires only one trick: the paper must be pleated—alternate folds are made forward and backward. You can use a standard sheet of copier paper and fold it neatly five times if you want to end up with five copies of your original. (You can make as many folds as you like, but the paper gets harder to cut, the more layers you have.)

Now it's time to draw. Find a pattern you like. Any illustration will do as long as the limbs of the person or animal you select will extend to the edges of your paper folds. Trace your illustration by smoothing a piece of tissue paper over the original and copying it line for line. Then use your tracing paper over a blank sheet of regular paper to transfer the pattern. If you're artistically inclined, you can draw your own paper doll. You can get as exotic as you like with a lion or an aardvark, a human or a Martian. Make sure that your figure goes right to the outside of the folds. You can also do internal cutouts in the center of your figure (for instance, a triangle or a heart) for added embellishment. When you've finished, unfold your pleats and voilà—your original has just multiplied many times over. You can now color in clothing or faces or whatever additional decoration you'd like.

What's even more fun, if you're a little more artistically inclined, is to create clothing for your dolls. (If you decide to do this, you'll have to cut the pleated figures apart.) You might want to design a trendy sweater and short skirt ensemble, or maybe uniforms for a sports team, with little tabs that you can fold around the dolls. You can even make wigs for your dolls, with different hairstyles to change with your mood.

Once you've got your gang ready to go, you can assign them names and personalities and have group therapy with everyone present. You may come up with some great solutions now that you don't have real people to deal with. This is one way to clear the air without making a phone call or confronting anyone. And if it works, keep those dolls around for an improptu conference whenever you need it. If you're worried about tearing or wrinkling them, you can always trace them onto a folded piece of felt.

91 ❃ String Me Along

In Greece, people play with worry beads. In the Navy, it's ball bearings. The idea of manipulating something between your fingers is a distraction—and can usually take your mind off your worries for at least twenty minutes. Cat's cradle can do the same thing, and it's infinitely variable. It will also keep you from engaging in some stress-related habit you are trying to avoid, like smoking, eating, or chewing your fingernails.

Just cut a piece of string about three feet in length and you've got a hot trip to a new place. Knot your string and stretch it over your hands so that a piece crosses the palm of each hand, looping around the pinky and thumb. You're now ready to play a few basic one-person cat's cradle games.

Bowl and Plate

Begin with the opening position. Run your right index finger under the flat line of string on your left palm and move your hands apart until the string is tight. Repeat with your left index finger. Bring your thumbs over the near index strings, then under the far index strings. Bring the strings toward you (each thumb should have two loops). With your teeth, lift the lower loop and bring it over your thumbs (this technique is called Navajo). Drop the pinky loops, and let your thumbs pull out their loops to extend the bowl and plate.

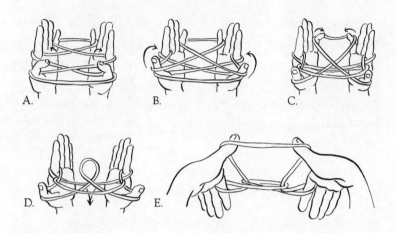

The Butterfly

From the bowl and plate, put your thumbs into the index loops (up into the plate) so that you end up with two loops on each thumb. Navajo the bottom thumb loop. Let your index fingers hook over the long string that crosses the middle of the figure and then back down into the index loops. Turn your hands so that the palms face away from you (index loops will slip down your fingers). Now straighten your index fingers to extend the butterfly.

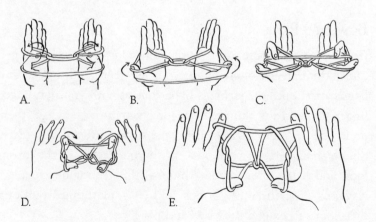

The Squeezer

Begin with the opening position. Turn your hands so that your thumbs are pointing up and your fingers away from you. Then rotate your hands inside the string loop until your thumbs are pointing down, touching the bottom string and your index fingers are pointing at one another.

Swing your thumbs under the bottom string making loops on your thumbs. Thumbs go under the near little finger string, and return. Pinkies go under the far thumb string, and return. From above, put your index fingers down into the loops

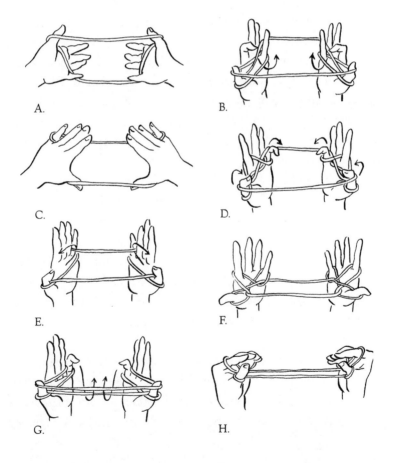

A.

B.

C.

D.

E.

F.

G.

H.

between your pinkies and thumbs and on the backs of those fingers, pick up the front palm strings.

Tip your thumbs down to let the upper straight thumb string slide off your thumbs (or Navajo it). Tip your pinkies down to let the upper straight pinky string slide off your pinkies (or Navajo it).

To make the squeezer squeeze, stretch your fingers open, then bring your fingers together. What a beautiful creation!

92 ❧ Summer Camp Fun

Lanyards remind us of the athletic side of life. If you went to camp, you must have made dozens of these to pass the time on rainy days. And what camp counselor or gym teacher didn't wear a lanyard necklace with a whistle attached so that he or she could stop a game in its tracks or call you up short on your mistakes? It's time for you to hark back to those vacations of yesteryear and make your own lanyard to wear as a bracelet, hang around your neck, or use on a keychain.

You'll need two laces at least three feet long of "gimp," or plastic cord, available in any craft shop. They come in great colors—you can even find sparkly ones. Choose two different colors. The skill of lanyard making lies in pulling the laces together so that each new weave is exactly as tight as the last one. The dedicated action of weaving the colors together gives you a whole new perspective on something useful to make with your own two hands. Use the drawings on pages 169–170 to guide you as you go through these steps.

Fold one of the laces in half and pinch the loop made by the fold. Hold the two ends in one hand and the loop in the other. Wind the loop all the way around the index finger of the hand in which you're holding the laces. Pinch the laces together where they cross to make a circle. Now slip the circle of lace off your finger and put the free end of the loop through it.

Slide the end of the second piece of gimp through the hole in the center of the knot. Pull this lace down to even it out (both laces should be the same length). Tighten the knot.

Hold the loop and the knot in one hand, with the loop hanging down. See step 6 in the drawing: A and C are of one color, B and D of the other.

You're going to make a square. Fold lace C over away from you to make a loop. Hold this lace with the same hand that holds the initial loop and knot, but put it between your index and middle fingers. Fold lace A toward you to make another loop. Next, thread B over the top of A and under C; then weave D over the top of C and under A. Pull the resulting cross tight by holding one lace between each thumb and index finger and tucking the other two into the curve between your other fingers and palms. As you pull, it should look like four little squares inside one big one.

To repeat the same pattern, keep looping just as you did in your first round. To change the pattern, reverse the strands (i.e.,

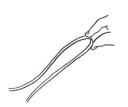  

1. Fold the lace so there is a loop. Give it a little pinch at the top to make he loop flat.

2. Hold the laces in one hand and the loop in the other.

3. Wind the loop all the way around the index finger of the hand that's holding the laces. Pinch the laces together where they cross to make a circle.

4. Slip the circle of lace off your finger. Put the free end of the loop through the circle. This is called an overhand knot.

5. Slide the other lace through the hole in the center of the knot. Pull this lace through until both laces are the same length.

6. Hold the loop and the knot upside down in one hand.

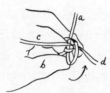

7. Fold lace C away from you to make a loop.

8. Fold lace A toward you to make another loop.

9. Thread lace B over the top of lace A and under lace C; weave lace D over the top of lace C and under lace A.

10. Pull each lace all the way through.

11. Continue to make side-by-side loops.

12. To finish, tie off two of the laces with regular knots and trim the ends.

13. Slip one end through the loop and tie and overhand knot. Trim the ends.

on the subsequent even rounds, B and D make the first loop; on the subsequent odd rounds, A and C make the first loop).

When you've had enough, tie off two of the laces with a knot, and then trim the ends. Use the other two laces to make the fastening. Slip one end through the loop, then use both ends to tie an overhand knot. You can attach a whistle or a keychain in the loop if you like. And in only twenty minutes, you've come up with a distinctive touch to your personal artifacts that no one else will have. Better than a book of snapshots, a lanyard will offer fond memories of a great twenty-minute vacation.

10
Where the Wild Things Are

Interacting with furry creatures helps lower your blood pressure, and dealing with a variety of other species teaches you a great deal about yourself. Rather than braving swamps and deserts, try your own safari a little closer to home.

93 ❧ Swim with the Goldfish

Fish, sequestered in their quiet tanks, have no problems. They have nothing to do, and nowhere to go, which is why watching them swim can be such a terrific stress reliever. An aquarium is a relatively cheap vacation investment, but if you're uncertain as to whether you might want to delve in, you can take this vacation in a pet store or a city aquarium.

Begin your trip by mentally entering into the undersea world of a tank. Imagine what it would be like to climb in and shed your limbs. All you have is fins and a tail, with gills that allow water and oxygen to pass in and out. Now you are in a completely protected space. The water, warmed to seventy-eight or eighty degrees Farenheit, is a perfect temperature. The hum of the motor is soothing, and the lively array of bubbles coming from the filters and the bubble stone lifts the spirits. Fish must be content in there, or at least they must feel no pressure. And you can share this experience, by allowing the complete calm of the fish to permeate your own spirit.

This is not to say that fish don't have fun. Watch how they chase one another through the tank—bumping up against the glass, reaching for food pellets, guzzling water. The larger the fish (an Oscar, or a big goldfish or cichlid, for example), the less playful it may be, but the more watchful and meditative. The smaller the fish, the more likely that you will see a school of them at once. Amazing how they stay in line, zipping here and there without breaking formation.

Time stops in a fish tank. The longer you watch, the more you see how fish fill the moments, whether they are lying low like a pleko or catfish, hanging suspended in water like an angelfish, or racing around just for the feeling of droplets coursing along their bodies like tetras.

Be a fish. Don't think, but rather, feel what it's like to let the water hold you and carry you along. Try to imagine what it would be like to have no night and day (except for the light fluctuation when the switch is on or off) and to have no responsibilities. You might open your mouth to experience a crumb of food or swallow of H_2O. If you perceive other fish around you, it will be only by sensor. Rather than being aware of personalities, as we are when we live with other people, you'll be honing in on their proximity. A kind of nonshocking electric current tells you that some other life form is near.

Where do you want to go in the tank? There are probably rocks and shells in which you could hide or around which you could dart. You might like to sink to the bottom and hang out on the pebbles, enjoying the dark and the sensation of relaxation that lying down offers. Or you might like to swim all the way to the top near the light, perhaps touching some plants, real or fake, that serve as decor in your tank. It might be fun to crowd up against the bubble stone and feel the spray hitting your scales, or to swim near the heater and see how the change of temperature affects your mood.

As your vacation ends, start to separate your own personality from that of the fish. Stand back now, and watch the inhabitants of the tank moving together or apart, circling aimlessly or with purpose. Can you make a comparison to your own life? Do you sometimes feel as though you're patterned by your environment—the people you live or work with, the things you've accumulated over the years, the house or office you spend so much time in?

Being a person means that you can absorb whatever you need from your environment, yet establish your own place, your own fun, outside the confines of whatever or whomever you spend time with.

As you turn away from the tank, take a deep breath and then let it out. Your world has just expanded, thanks to the fish.

94 ❧ A Visit with Mother Nature

A spiderweb is a thing of beauty, an amazing, strong, architecturally magnificent structure that is the lifework of the female of the species. We all wish that we could create something meaningful, something useful, and taking a vacation to watch a spider work can be inspiring.

What is a web, anyway? It's a construct of one piece connected to another and another, branching out as far as it has to go. A determined group of spiders, it seems, could create a web that stretched to infinity. The World Wide Web was inspired by this small creature and her work—and you may spend enough time on the technological counterpart to hold a spider's web in total awe. Imagine making one of those things anytime you wanted.

Once you've spotted the master craftswoman you wish to apprentice with, you should have no trouble seeing the process in action. First, she'll find her location. It could be anywhere: the underside of a porch, a doorway, or swung between a couple of trees like a hammock. The spider's spinnerets, located in sacs on the underside of her abdomen, produce a fibrous protein fluid, an exocrine or glandular secretion that looks like silk. It is stronger than steel and more useful, because it's elastic.

Any spider can spin—even those trapped in a space capsule can do it in zero gravity. From one strand, then the next and the next, a seemingly haphazard pattern begins to take on ever widening octagons, pentagons, or decahedrons from a central point. Watch how patiently she weaves, getting everything just right, leaving spaces where they should be, erecting then removing pieces of her scaffolding with a combination of sticky and nonsticky threads. She continues back and forth over weak pieces until they have just the shape and form she wants.

Spiders can form draglines too, to help them find their way along a path, and to guard them from falls. The young ones often put out silk parachutes, tethering themselves by one thread to a rooted spot and then letting the wind carry them for miles.

What can this type of perseverance and planning tell you about your own work? Of course, you're on vacation now, but you probably remember days when you would sit around trying to get your project started. You'd go off in a couple of hundred different directions, make a few distracting phone calls, have a lot of coffee, check your E-mail, and do any number of things that might get you off track. If you were a spider and you acted that way, you probably wouldn't eat. Because, of course, the web is beautiful, but it has a purpose: it is the ultimate food-gathering tool for the intrepid spider.

How fortunate that nature is always combining form and function. All a spider has to do is weave, and the bugs come right to her doorstep: moths flying too low, tiny crawling bugs who don't know better, a couple of ants who got stuck in their pilgrimage after their own food.

When the web is completely finished, the spider may sit back and examine her handiwork, or she may go out into the world. Look at what she's done. The web glistens with dew in the morning light; it bars the way for other creatures that might step in its path; it seduces bugs in the vicinity to come and climb on its sticky surface. The web links trees and leaves; it withstands thunder and rain. And if it's destroyed by an animal or human lumbering along, the spider doesn't care. The purpose of this one web has been served, and it's time to move on.

If you have appreciated the enormity of the web and every-thing it can do, you may also have started to understand that whatever you make or do is not permanent. It's good to have been there and done that, but you can't get attached because once your project or product exists, it's no longer yours. Just like the spider's web, it belongs to everyone.

This trip should open your eyes, not only to the world of nature, but also to your sense of wonder for what you can make and what you can leave.

95 ❊ Go Squirrely

When you're feeling as if the world is just too much, take a break and go watch squirrels. You can do this in your own backyard, in a park, or even on the streets of small towns. Those adorable little rodents are everywhere, and they're ready to serve as your tour guide when you want to take a trip outside your own four walls.

What you're going to do on this vacation is watch the behavior of squirrels and figure out what it is they have that you lack. And then you're going to adapt the qualities of squirrelness that you particularly like to your own life.

First of all, squirrels are incredibly active and industrious little creatures. You rarely see them sitting still, unless they are playing hide-and-seek and waiting for their partner to discover them. They seem to dart rather than walk, using their tenacious paws to scamper along railings and fences, up and down trees, flipping upside down and backward in order to get where they're going. If they come upon a piece of food, they'll take it even if they're not hungry, stuffing their cheeks to the bursting point so that they'll have something for later. Squirrels think ahead.

Make a mental note now of what you might mimic about a squirrel's exercise regimen and conservation program. Do you tend to sit around during the day and think about doing an hour at the gym? Do you make lists instead of going out and getting or doing what you really have a yen for? After this trip, you're going to attack problems in a much more direct fashion—just like a squirrel.

Now think about squirrel relationships. When you hear the distinctive cries of a squirrel, it usually has something to do with either location, danger, mating, or parenting. Squirrels make great moms. They find a place for their pups to be safe, they nurse and protect them, and their scent makes their kids feel safe and secure. What is also significant about good relations between the generations is the amount of touch the mothers give their babies. They are constantly in contact. When a mother squirrel licks her baby, it stimulates the production of growth hormone. And the comfort of being in a nest, crowded up against squirrel siblings and parents, is an inducement for the young to eat, drink, and develop normally.

On your vacation, think about how much touching you generally do during the day. Did you hug your kids when you left the house? Did you snuggle up against your significant other last night? How much do you embrace your friends and relatives? What we can learn from the squirrels is that the power of touch is more than magical—it provides the human connection that makes us want to get up in the morning and seize the day. A vacation filled with good touch for you and yours—just like the squirrels—can make the difference between chronic stress and an ability to ride out the worst of the storm.

So go home and imagine yourself waving your bushy tail and setting your beady little eyes upon the one you love. Then hug, snuggle, kiss, tickle, and grab for all you're worth. Like a squirrel gathering nuts for a long winter, you can store up plenty of good feelings and a lot of pleasure.

96 ✻ Feline Happy Time

Cats will do anything to rub up against stuff. Watch them roll around in the dirt, clean their whiskers with their tongues, rub up against a piece of furniture. It's as if the entire cat body is hungry for sensation. If you have a cat, you know that there's no way you can win when she goes after something she wants, especially when what she wants is for you to massage her thoroughly and well.

Taking a vacation with your cat can be a curiously bonding event, since cats tend to be independent and don't hang around soaking up attention, like dogs. Having this twenty minutes together will offer both of you the opportunity to get closer. Although the vacation appears on the surface to be designed for your cat, it's really the ultimate hedonistic escape for you. After all, you get to cuddle up to fur, luxuriate in the sun, and feel you're doing a good deed for your pet.

Pick a location where the two of you can be completely comfortable: it might be a blanket on your patio or a comfy chair on a side porch. You will need to approach your cat at the right moment. She has to be either sleepy or doing that I-know-everything-in-the-world cat stare as she sits calmly on whatever piece of furniture she has designated as her throne.

Gently pick her up and carry her to your vacation spot. Put her in your lap or right beside you, and rest your hand on her body to establish your connection. Your touch should be light but firm, so as not to startle or upset her. Move your hand in the direction of her fur, starting with her head and working your way down her body. She will probably respond to your touch, offering a part of herself to be massaged. If she doesn't, keep stroking, making sure you cover her head, neck, belly, and back. Most animals don't enjoy having their paws touched, but yours may be the exception. Work the muscles around the collarbones and ribs, being careful to respect your cat's appreciation of what you're doing. (If she stops purring or starts pulling away, you're digging in too hard.)

While you're working, pay attention to the cat's behavior and attitude. How many of us can be that relaxed, can get into pleasure so deeply that the rest of the world and its concerns just vanish? Think of the cat as your teacher of stress management: the more time you spend absorbing her calm demeanor, her blissful repose, the more you'll be able to sit quietly in the sun without her, doing nothing.

97 ❊ Rover's Hoop Dreams

Stupid pet tricks are actually more beneficial for the pet owner than the pet. When we teach a dog, cat, monkey, or parrot to do something totally ridiculous, we are able to reestablish our alpha dominance over the animal kingdom (thereby making ourselves feel important and smart). In addition, people will stop us on the street and ask, "Where did you get that brilliant dog (cat, monkey, parrot)?" and we'll be able to say that the poor creature was nothing before it met us but has blossomed into a very Einstein on all fours.

Before you can do the hoop thing, your pet must already know basic commands such as sit, stay, down, and come. It makes no sense to teach a puppy who is jumping all over you with muddy paws to jump through a hoop, because jumping is jumping—that is, you will continue to be annoyed by the bad behavior. Once you have a reasonable pet that speaks your language fairly well (as long as there is a treat on the other end of the command), you're in business.

You will need a hula hoop, which you can purchase at most toy stores, and a second human, who will assist in the teaching process. Since twenty minutes is all the attention span you'll get from most pets (and most people), each step of the process will constitute one twenty-minute safari vacation. This means that you actually have several vacations all wrapped up in one, kind of like a time-share in Aruba where you go to enjoy "your" property a few times a year.

Start your first outing by placing the hoop within a door frame so that it touches the floor. Put your pet on a leash, and have your partner call the animal by name: "Come, Archibald!" You then lead the pet through the hoop by passing the leash back and forth with your partner. Each of you will offer a small treat as a reward at the beginning and praise him to the heavens. When your pet has accomplished this step, move on to repeating the activity with no leash, using only the "come" command. Pretty soon, that dog, cat, monkey, or parrot will be moving right along through the hoop. When the animal is responding regularly, you can offer treats only some of the time.

Some pets just don't get it right away. If yours is one, don't be frustrated or think you have a pet that needs remedial reading or physical therapy. It's possible that you have a really intelligent pet who thinks that this exercise is too dumb to bother with. Deal with it and laugh. Remember, you're on vacation.

But if your pet is going right through the hoop on a regular basis, you can move on to more difficult assignments. Your next outing involves lifting the hoop slightly off the floor and encouraging your pet to come through. Be sure to adjust the size of the hoop to your pet's size; very smart pets, such as cats, will sneak right underneath. Why should they do something in order to please you? This is no vacation for the pet, understand.

One of you humans may need to crouch down and prevent this avoidance tactic by waving your hands frantically or possibly throwing a toy mouse through the hoop, which the cat will pursue at all costs.

Finally, you'll take the hoop out of the door frame and place it in the middle of the floor. Go back to leash work, reminding the pet exactly where it's supposed to go. Use the "come" command, and persuade the animal to jump right through the center.

On the final outings, you'll work without the leash and without a treat. Keep your voice upbeat and delighted, and *praise, praise, praise* each time the pet makes it through the hoop.

More advanced vacations call for a ring of fire, which would provide the same level of adventure as a real safari, but these are not recommended for the average pet enthusiast. And your flight insurance doesn't cover it, either.

98 ✷ Jungle Journey

You've had it. You want to get as far from civilization as possible. But maybe you have a pile of work on your desk, children to care for, or in-laws coming for dinner. What better escape than a trip in your mind to the ends of the earth—courtesy of some good wildlife audiotapes? These can be purchased at many bookstores, at some large pet stores, and at natural history museum gifts hops.

For twenty minutes, you are going to vanish in the veld, track a tiger, examine an elephant. Put on your headphones, connect up to your CD player or tape recorder, and you're ready to go.

Close your eyes and picture the scene. You are very warm, starting to perspire, but it's early morning, and you are filled with energy. Decide where you'd like to be. Have you always imagined yourself in Africa, about to charge with a rough-and-ready rhino? Or are you more the swamp type, eager to paddle downriver with a cranky crocodile? Once you've selected your site, visualize yourself dressed for the event. You want to be protected—be sure you're wearing sunscreen and a hat. You also need good walking shoes and light clothing. You may be trekking many miles up mountains and across rocks.

Now settle in and really listen to the tape. You can hear the call of some huge animal in the distance, while around you are the clamor of small creatures—maybe a few monkeys swing through the trees, providing the *whoosh* of a vine as it clears your head. Feel the softness of grass or deep mud under your feet. See what it's like to be really alone, deep in the woods or along the banks of a wide river. You must step carefully and be completely aware of everything around you. Danger lurks, but at the same time, it's enthralling and challenging to be right in the center of a world not of your making. You are a visitor here and must honor the customs of the birds and beasts around you.

Listen. Is it day or night? Is the weather fine or inclement? What kinds of sounds should alert you to danger? Which ones appear to be compelling calls for help or attraction, and which are just the background score of this natural symphony? Do you have a feeling that you'd like to stay, riveted to the spot, or is it time to move on and return to your rarified, civilized life?

Remove the headphones, and take a minute to regain your equilibrium. You will now hear the click of computer keys, the buzz of conversation or, if you're at home, the hum of the washer or dryer and the ring of the telephone. The question remains, Which life is more real? Is it the one you have here, with your eyes open, or the one you just glimpsed with your eyes closed? Did you travel to a land in your vacation that can teach you something powerful about yourself and where you fit in the context of time and space?

Remember that what you heard through those headphones is not a dream; somewhere out there, it exists. And for a brief few moments, you were part of it.

99 ❀ Backyard Birding

Alfred Hitchcock scared us all half to death with the movie *The Birds*, but most of us have a fond place in our hearts for the little creatures that fly overhead like poetry in motion or search for worms in the early morning. On this trip, you're going to attract birds, identify them, and examine their behavior.

No matter where you live, you live with birds. On the busiest city streets, pigeons strut their stuff. In enclaves behind buildings, shopping malls, and tourist attractions, sparrows can be seen jumping to and fro, pecking for food. There are seagulls and Canada geese where you least expect them, blue jays that screech their heads off, and cardinals that make their brief crimson appearance at backyard barbecues.

Imagine that you are a city dweller, in search of a respite in the midst of your busy day. Go outside, and you will immediately be struck by the gangs of pigeons darting away from cars and waddling around baby strollers. Select one pigeon and watch him doing his thing. If you live in the suburbs or the country, you will probably select a sparrow or a blue jay. (If you are fortunate and live near water, you might spy a blue heron standing heroically on one leg, waiting for a fish to come by.)

The bird you select will be your companion on this journey. What does he look like? What distinguishes him from his brothers? It may be the odd shape of his beak, or the distinctive markings on his head. How large is he in comparison with his fellows? Does his plumage seem shiny and well kept, or is he bedraggled, the feathers lying in a haphazard pattern against his body? Is he all puffy, little bits of him falling out as he cleans himself? This might mean he's seriously advanced in age. Is he quick and small, trying hard to compete for food with larger birds? Maybe he's just a chick.

Now spend some time observing his behavior. He cocks his head, fixes his beady eyes on whatever interests him, and quickly flutters off if you get too close. Most birds can roost for hours, unmoving. Even a pigeon seems calm when he does this, emitting such a delightful "coo" that you would swear this fine-feathered friend is a perennial favorite instead of a "garbage bird" or "a rat with wings," as some people call them!

Watch the flight of the bird. Some will light on a hedge, then zoom down onto the grass or pavement; they may dive-bomb other birds when they're in peril of losing a precious bit of food. Others are unconcerned about anything but the grace and speed of getting off the ground and staying there. It is magical to think that something heavier than air can glide so easily. What would it be like if you were a bird and suddenly had the ability to take flight?

How do you attract a bird to come close? You'll need food, of course, but you may not be able to lure a reluctant sparrow or jay in only twenty minutes. You can try throwing down a piece of food (anything from bread to french fries) and see what happens. Sometimes just staying still and quiet is your best bet. Even if you don't see a bird, you can usually hear one, because it's hard for them to be silent. The constant chatter has to do with finding a location, avoiding danger, mating, and finding food. Those are the major activities when you're a bird.

If you've just missed a bird, you'll usually find a feather. Amazing the range and delicacy of these colorful banners of bird-hood. End your vacation by collecting a souvenir. Pick up a feather, and keep it with you for the day. When you pick one up, it may appear torn or bent, its fronds separated out from one another. But run it through your fingers, and it returns to form— and is, once again, a thing of beauty.

100 ❧ People Watching

Tracking a wild beast isn't something you can do easily in twenty minutes. You might crave the sight of a bear, a deer, a fox, or even a possum or raccoon, but it's not awfully practical. Remember, however, that there's one species you can detect and follow all you want, if you're discreet. That species is *Homo sapiens*.

This vacation is a variation on eavesdropping and can be an entertaining diversion if you're not found out. What you're going to do is walk around on your lunch hour and find an interesting individual to study. On nice days, many workers spend their lunch breaks sitting by the fountain in front of their building, or in a park across the street. So, what you're going to

do is select a person and track the subjects movements, idio-
syncrasies, behavior—and even diet!

First pick a good spot for viewing. Anywhere near a large
pool of people will do. Before you throw yourself into this vacation, you must know a little about covering your tracks. After
all, you don't want to be detected. Make sure you have some
ostensible activity to keep you busy: reading the newspaper,
talking on a cell phone (you don't really have to dial), or eating
lunch. If the subject of your attention notices your interest, simply look away or begin to concentrate on someone else. You can
always turn back in a few minutes.

Now let your eyes scan the crowd. At first, you'll see dozens
of white shirts, T-shirts, high heels, purses, briefcases, and faces.
It's the faces you want to hone in on because what we carry
inside us is usually revealed by the expression and emotion contained in the face. What kind of visage appeals to you? Are you
looking for someone supremely confident and delighted with
life? Are you looking for someone who is a little sad and maybe
could use a bit of cheering up? Do you want someone you might
emulate in your own style, or someone who is so foreign to
your way of being and thinking that he or she might as well
come from another planet?

Having settled on the type of person you want to study, you
need to zero in on the specific individual. There! Let your gaze
lie lightly on this person, and see what you can fathom about
her. Is she tall or short, fat or thin? Is she alone or with a friend?
Can you tell what she does for a living by the way she's dressed
or the way she carries herself?

See how she moves. It's always intriguing to watch a person
who is comfortable in her body, who is nicely aligned and
effortlessly maintains a straight spine and a head held high. It's
also compelling to see someone who has a limitation or handi-

cap but manages surely, as though nothing were in any way different or impaired.

Watch the way she eats. Some people eat as if they'll never get enough; others as though it were a guilty pleasure. You can tell when there's real enjoyment in her face or when she's just munching to pass the time and fill her stomach. Does she tear right into her lunch, or does she take her time, having a conversation first or enjoying the freedom of being away from her desk, just like you?

It's fun imagining what the rest of her life must be like. Who knows what's going on in her mind right now, at this very moment. Feel, for a moment, just like her. As you identify with this multifaceted creature who is now a part of your fantasy life, you can create a world around her. She might be having a mad affair with a younger man, or have a son who's just moved to Japan, or she might be considering quitting her job so that she can take a permanent vacation.

Now see how she begins the process of starting back to work. You will notice whether she glances at her watch or just casually gets up and discards the remains of her lunch, then lingers on the street or maybe decides to take a walk somewhere. Does she seem to go with the flow—starting back when her colleagues do—or is she a loner, maybe a person with an errand to run or a phone call to make before it's time to return to work?

It's endlessly engaging, watching the species you've selected. This type of wildlife is never, ever boring.

Coda:
Taking Your Vacation
Home with You

We have all had the experience of going away for a week or two and returning to find the answering machine full of messages, the mail piled up on the doorstep, and life ready to smack us in the face. We've worked so hard at getting mellow, and then, within just a day—even an hour—we find it's as though we never left. We're back in the rat race, scrambling to make up for lost time.

Let me tell you how to keep your twenty-minute vacation with you throughout the day. Once you've got the secret, you will start to find that you are getting more out of your vacations, and you are enjoying your time away completely.

Plan to take a vacation as soon as you get up in the morning. Even if you don't know what you'll be in the mood for later on, pick a time at which you will drop everything and take your trip. Make a date with yourself that you cannot break, and put it on your calendar. As the time approaches, select a category, and about an hour before, pick the exact vacation. This is just like booking with your travel agent: remember that you get charged if you cancel! In addition, you can anticipate how much fun you're going to have in just a little while.

When your vacation is over and you're on your way back to the real world, give some thought as to what actually happened to you on the trip. Did you learn something about yourself: how relaxed or distracted you get, why you fight with yourself about taking time off, what thoughts and emotions this vacation has prompted that relate to the rest of your life? Then make a connection between whatever you got out of your journey and what you have to do for the rest of the day.

When you have figured the connection, no matter what goes on for the next twenty-four hours, hold it in your mind and spirit. Recall the trip you took and what it meant while you were in the midst of it. Keep asking yourself how you can transfer the smile that it put on your face or the harmony that it put in your soul to all the other things you have to do in life.

Vacations give us a time away from chores, but they are not a true escape. We take ourselves with us wherever we go. However, in structuring these brief periods of complete enjoyment in our day, we give ourselves a gift. When we know beyond a doubt that it's possible to let go on vacation, we can begin to trigger a relaxation response even when we're back.

Now you can abandon the frantic scurry for more time off. Use every single moment as break time, and you'll be on the right track all day, every day.

◡: Index :◡

About the Author

J udith Sachs, the daughter and granddaughter of physicians, has been writing and teaching about stress management for the past decade. The author of over twenty books on preventive healthcare, including *Break the Stress Cycle* and *Sensual Rejuvenation*, she frequently speaks and writes about relaxation and re-energizing techniques at colleges and universities, holistic health centers, in corporate settings, and on national television and radio programs.

Judith has served on the faculty of the Omega Institute for Holistic Studies, New York's Open Center, Canyon Ranch in the Berkshires, the New Age Health Spa, the Spa at Grand Lake, and the College of New Jersey. She has created two ongoing courses on stress management and life/work balance for the Human Resources Development Institute of New Jersey. She has also appeared as a health expert on such shows as "Leeza," "Good Day New York," the "Phil Donahue Show," the "Susan Powter Show," "Rolanda," "Jenny Jones," and "Today/Weekend Edition." A long-time practitioner of the Chinese art of tai chi chuan, Sachs teaches privately as well as at senior centers throughout central New Jersey.